CONTENTS

TABLES AND EXAMPLES

Acknowledgements

The Schools Council wishes to thank all those who provided data for the
research, particularly the staff of the nine schools which participated
in the detailed study, whose co-operation and constructive criticism
made this report possible.

Thanks are also due from the author to members of the project steering
group: Lesley Kant, Keith Weller, Joan Leake, Geoff Bardell, Brian
Goacher, Alma Craft and Peter Herbert, whose general oversight and helpful
contributions were greatly appreciated.

PROFILE REPORTS
FOR SCHOOL-LEAVERS

Janet Balogh

LONGMAN FOR SCHOOLS COUNCIL

1982

Published by Longman for Schools Council
Longman Resources Unit
33-35 Tanner Row
York YO1 1JP

1 INTRODUCTION

Readers of the British press in 1980 might well have believed that the country was united in calling for the introduction of profile reports, even if it was not clear what this entailed. The same readers would also have been forgiven for believing that every other school in the country was introducing profile reporting. The need to encourage schools to concentrate on the development of basic skills and practical subjects, and the belief that profile reports would improve motivation by encouraging pupils to take part in their own assessment were oft-mentioned justifications. It was also suggested that examinations provided insufficient information about the abilities of school-leavers, even for those who succeeded in a wide range of subjects.

The majority of school-leavers have an examination certificate as documentary evidence of their five years of secondary schooling (in 1979 78% gained a Certificate of Secondary Education (CSE) or General Certificate of Education Ordinary (O level graded result) in English; the corresponding figure for mathematics was 68%[1]); and many schools provide references and/or testimonials to augment this information. However, Her Majesty's Inspectorate (HMI) pointed out (1980): '... there is as yet no assured meaning, locally or nationally, to be attached to the statement that a school leaver has completed the basic cycle of secondary education, beyond the fact that he [sic] has stayed till 16.'[2]

Indeed, the desirability of a published school record had been advocated by many educationists from the Second World War onwards (Norwood Report, 1943;[3] Beloe Report, 1960;[4] Schools Council, 1975;[5] Finniston Report, 1980[6]). During the late 1970s there was a concerted plea for a detailed document which would provide full information on an individual school-leaver's competences, experience and interests. Ironically, in the 1950s, local education authorities (LEAs) had offered leaving certificates which provided some of this information but the introduction of the CSE led to their withdrawal in most cases.

The Warnock Report (1978) suggested the purpose of education should be: '... to enlarge a child's knowledge, experience and imaginative understanding, and ... awareness of moral values and capacity for enjoyment; to enable him to enter the world after formal education is over as an active participant in society and a responsible contributor to it, capable of achieving as much independence as possible.'[7] Similar views were expounded in HMI's *Aspects of Secondary Education in England*. '... schools should promote valuable personal and intellectual qualities such as curiosity, the ability to express views orally, the capacity to work as a member of a team and to work independently.'[8] The public examination system undoubtedly emphasizes cognitive abilities rather than personal and social skills; many educationists would wish the examination influence to be less pervasive. At present the curriculum of fourth and fifth year pupils is often dominated by the need to cover an examination syllabus and this may leave little time for the development of other skills and qualities.

The pressure on schools to document and record personal and social skills extends beyond the world of education. John Raven in *Education, Values and Society*[9] suggests that employers, parents and pupils would all welcome this. Some schools already make great efforts to ensure that their pupils are well prepared for adult life, and keep detailed records of their students' development, but the expectation seems to be that if Raven's 'life-useful competences' are assessed and recorded all schools will be obliged to provide opportunities for all pupils to develop them. In this way a profile report could exert a broadening effect on the fourth and fifth year curriculum and so go some way towards lessening the specialization which the examination system tends to encourage.

Government politicians and organizations such as the Confederation of British Industry (CBI) and Manpower Services Commission (MSC) have also shown interest in the idea of profile reports and the development of understanding of the world outside school. Neil Kinnock, speaking for the Labour Party, suggested each school-leaver should have a profile which would be written by teachers and which would provide information about the pupil's development and character.[10] The MSC's director of training wanted pupils to leave school with the basic skills of reading, writing and arithmetic but also with an appreciation (among other things) of the need to work consistently, quickly and accurately and to arrive punctually.[11] Profile reports are seen by many as a means by which schools can make their detailed knowledge of their pupils available to careers officers, further education establishments and employers.

In its evidence to the Commons Select Committee on Education, Science and Arts the CBI stated that 'School examinations are too academic and do not assess qualities highly valued by employers', and that it 'strongly supported the development of pupil profiles, recording academic, practical and personal strengths and weaknesses, particularly social and communications skills which conventional examinations were not designed to evaluate'.[12]

Various suggestions have been made about the form such documents should take. The Scottish Council for Research in Education[13] advocates recording teachers' assessments of pupils' attainments, basic skills and personal qualities to give a comprehensive picture of their aptitudes and interests. The Further Education Curriculum Review and Development Unit (FEU) suggests that pupils and teachers should discuss the assessments, and 'to provide for the sometimes conflicting requirements of validity, reliability, flexibility, comparability, competence grading, experience recording and formative assessment, the Study Group is of the opinion that a form of profile reporting which incorporates some grading will be necessary'.[14]

Tyrrell Burgess and Betty Adams[15] believe that both the fourth and fifth year curricula should be a matter for negotiation between tutor (teacher) and pupil. They hope this will provide the basis for a statement by the school-leaver about his/her school experience which would be externally moderated and have currency in the community. Patricia

Broadfoot[16] would also like to see the development of pupil self-assessment go further 'to balance the alienative effects of such [external] evaluation and to encourage motivation by helping pupils to find their studying more fulfilling in itself.'

This public discussion and support for public records for school-leavers has been accompanied by initiatives in a small number of schools, a selection of which form the subject of this report. Other schools have reorganized their extant recording systems to provide more information for references and testimonials for school-leavers. Schools are well aware that it is not easy for their leavers to obtain employment and are anxious to do all they can to help place their students in suitable jobs.

However, the interest shown in school-leaving statements by the press, pressure groups and political parties is only matched by the general lack of agreement over the meaning of the term 'profile'. It may be used to describe an internal school assessment which includes information on personal qualities, or a pupil-compiled document which may reveal personal qualities and experiences, but the term is more often used to describe a record which gives information about a wide range of a pupil's attributes. A profile report might include estimated public examination results, levels of competence in basic language and arithmetic skills, assessments of cross-curricular skills such as listening, speaking, manual dexterity, problem-solving, and personal qualities such as initiative and perseverance.

In practice, these documents have many names and this creates further confusion. Leavers' Certificate, Fifth Form Certificate, School Leaving Report, Leaver's Profile Report, School Testimonial, School Diploma, Record of Achievement and Personal Achievement Record are all used as titles for public documents which provide more or less comprehensive statements of pupils' educational experiences, competences and interests at the end of their period of compulsory education.

2 DOCUMENTARY INFORMATION ABOUT SCHOOL-LEAVERS

THE RANGE OF PRESENT PRACTICE

Most sixteen-year-old school-leavers will have one or more public examination certificates and perhaps a collection of school reports. Most also have the opportunity to ask their school for a testimonial and/or a reference. These documents may not provide timely, appropriate or sufficient information for diagnosis and discussion of strengths and weaknesses or for decision-making about, or placement in, employment, youth opportunity schemes or further education. Even where they may provide a comprehensive and informative picture of a particular school-leaver they may not be automatically provided for all the year group. They may also be so individual as to preclude comparisons between pupils.

In the vast majority of schools in England and Wales, a testimonial, reference or school report is the major source of information about a prospective employee or student. School reports vary in format and style, but they are generally written for parents and pupils rather than employers. Many teachers use fifth year reports to point out weaknesses as well as strengths; they are intended to help pupils improve their performance and, where applicable, achieve the best possible results in public examinations. Reports, therefore, may be used as a focus of discussion about future plans and hopes but they do not necessarily supply the details employers and FE colleges want, and they are certainly not usually written with these audiences in mind.

Testimonial and reference writing tends to be a time-consuming part of the job of a senior member of staff, often the fifth year tutor, deputy head or head. In some schools testimonials are written on request while in others they are automatically prepared for all leavers. They may include grades for attendance and punctuality and may be closely based on detailed records kept throughout a pupil's stay in the school, but at some periods of the school year they may have to be written more hurriedly to meet deadlines.

The careers service and some employers may send their own forms to schools for completion. They find it more convenient to have all the required information in a familiar format, which also permits easy comparison of candidates from several schools. Filling in these documents may be as time-consuming as writing references, and they have the added disadvantage that several may be needed for any one pupil, each requiring slightly different information.

References and the forms completed for the careers service and employers are generally confidential. The contents may be discussed in general terms with pupils and parents but they are not the property of the school-leaver. However, some schools have introduced profile reports so that school-leavers will have a document which complements the more usual public examination certificate and reference. Some of these profile report schemes have been seminal and are reviewed below.

In 1973, concerned about the divisiveness of the external examination system, the Headteachers' Association of Scotland decided to 'consider the manner and range of assessments in secondary schools that might result in a form of report or certificate applicable to all pupils completing [the 15-16 year-old level]'.[17] A working party developed an assessment and recording procedure which would provide information for discussion and guidance in school and lead to a leaving report for all pupils. This leaving report records teacher assessments of the skills listening, speaking, reading, writing, visual understanding and expression, use of number, physical co-ordination and manual dexterity, and personal qualities, enterprise and perseverance. Assessment is on a four-point scale and each grade represents approximately 25% of the year group. There is also a section for 'other observations' which includes details of 'school activities, other awards and comments on positive personal qualities'. This scheme has been much discussed and has influenced a number of other profile reports, such as Clydebank. However, even in Scotland it has not been widely adopted in the original form, and many schools which took part in the pilot scheme have dropped out, partly because it proved very time-consuming and partly because the cross-curricular assessment was a departure from tradition in Scotland, where subject-based teaching is the rule.

In Wales about a half dozen schools have been operating profile report schemes for some years. Brynmawr School, for example, has a detailed profile report which includes the results of literacy and numeracy tests, continuous assessment of communication skills, and qualities such as self-discipline and initiative. Deeside High School offers pupils a School Leaving Certificate which includes teacher assessment of qualities such as sociability and resilience; students are encouraged to include details of their participation in sports and community service.

Evesham High School, Hereford and Worcester, has developed a Personal Achievement Record for its fifth year.[18] This is a plastic-covered logbook issued to any fifth year pupil who asks the form tutor for it. The book has three sections: the first is for pupils to enter details of the courses they are following; the second section consists of lists of language, mathematical, practical and social skills; and the third section provides space for pupils to enter their personal achievements. When pupils believe they have mastered a skill listed in the second section, they ask an 'appropriate member of staff ... to authenticate [their] achievement'. The principle behind the scheme is that 'Pupils must initiate and staff must confirm positive statements of fact'.[19]

Outcomes of Education[15] describes some of the profile report schemes which involve pupils in assessing themselves. These include that of the Sutton Centre, Nottinghamshire, where pupils, staff and parents regularly complete subject reports which are kept to provide a complete profile of the pupil's school career; the work of Comberton Village College's English department, where pupils are asked to contribute their own views on their progress; and the work of Don Stansbury at Totnes.

Stansbury pioneered the *Record of Personal Achievement* (RPA) in

Swindon as a response to the anticipated needs of pupils affected by the raising of the school-leaving age from fifteen to sixteen (RoSLA). 'The aim of RPA was "the development of personal qualities" and it was hoped that the scheme would achieve such an aim by functioning in three ways:

(i)   it would provide an organizing principle for the work of certain pupils

(ii) it would help to motivate those pupils

(iii) it would provide at least the possibility of a leaving qualification for all pupils who participated.'[20]

Each pupil who participates in the RPA has a looseleaf file in which to store the cards on which he/she makes the record of day-to-day activities and achievements. Each entry is verified by an adult but there is no adult control of the entries apart from this. RPA was introduced into 4 pilot schools in September 1970 and by 1975 67 schools in 33 LEAs were operating the scheme. Stansbury developed the similar *Record of Personal Experience*[21] when he moved to Totnes School, Devon; this too is now used in other schools. In theory, pupils of all abilities can take part in the scheme but in practice it is mostly offered to non-examination pupils. The Schools Council thoroughly evaluated the RPA scheme,[22] and recently helped to fund the introduction of Personal Achievement into approximately 20 more schools in south and southwest England; one of the aims of this support is to make RPA available to pupils of all abilities.

Chapters 1 and 2 above suggest the diversity of thinking on profile reports and the possible range of models. However, apart from the few publicized examples, there appeared to be little tangible information about the range and extent of practice when in 1980 the Schools Council decided to survey the development of profile reports as part of its Programme Five, Improving the Examinations System. Chapter 3 describes the survey in detail.

3 SURVEY OF PUPIL PROFILES AT 16+

DESCRIPTION AND METHOD

The Schools Council survey was commissioned to consider:

1. the number of ·schools operating profile report schemes;

2. the nature of profile reports in use;

3. the reason for their introduction;

4. the assessment procedures employed in the profile reports;

5. the attitudes of those involved in the schemes.

The purpose of the study was to investigate more fully the claims made
for profile reports (in particular, whether they could provide an alternative qualification for sixteen-year-old school-leavers), to consider
their implications, and to make recommendations on good practice and
possible future developments. The survey was confined to England, as
the Schools Council's Committee for Wales, jointly with the Council's
Programme Two: Helping Individual Teachers to Become More Effective and
with the Welsh Joint Education Committee, was developing profile reports
for possible use in Welsh schools. Programme Two was also supporting
other profile reporting initiatives, for example, the dissemination of
the work on assessment profiles which was done at St Gregory's RC
Secondary School, Kirby, in Knowsley LEA.

The survey of profile reporting was to be completed within a year
(January-December 1981), so it was essential to identify and contact
schools offering profile report schemes very quickly. (The number of
schools offering profile reports proved to be comparatively small, hence
a 'random' sample, of some 20% of secondary schools in England, could
have missed them all as well as taking more time than was available.)
All the 104 English LEAs were sent a letter asking them to name schools
in their area operating profile report schemes. A follow-up letter was
sent when necessary and in some cases telephone reminders were also
given. The response is set out in Table 1. Schools Council Field
Officers, who work in regional areas, also supplied names of schools
involved in profile reporting. Some schools wrote direct to the Council
when they read about the project in the press or in the Council's
information materials.

All schools so identified were sent a brief questionnaire. Its
principle purpose was to identify 8-10 schools for detailed study and to
obtain additional information to illuminate the overall picture. The
level of response is set out in Table 2. Using LEAs as a filter was not
altogether successful. They are under considerable pressure from
researchers and faced with many requests for information. It became
clear that they are not always aware of the nature of the initiatives in

Table 1 LEA response to request to name schools with profile report
         schemes

	No.	%
LEAs supplying names of schools	42	*41*
LEAs replying that they had no schools operating profile reports	43	*41*
No response	19	*18*
LEAs contacted	104	*100*

Table 2 School responses to questionnaire

	No.	%
Schools completing and returning questionnaires	75	*55*
Schools replying no profile report scheme in operation	39	*29*
No response	21	*16*
Schools contacted	135	*100*

their schools. The reply of one headmaster to the questionnaire was not untypical: 'I was not aware before the receipt of your letter of 19 May that my school was operating a profile report system and, therefore, I do not think I will be able to help you.'

When the completed questionnaires were analysed and the documents accompanying them studied, the need for a more precise definition of profile reports became apparent. For the purposes of the study it was decided that the kinds of profile report which would yield the most comprehensive and pertinent information and make it more possible at the end of the study to offer recommendations on good practice and future work would meet the following criteria.

1. The profile report should record the assessment of skills and/or qualities besides traditional subject attainment, such as assessment of basic mathematical and language skills, cross-curricular skills such as listening and problem-solving, practical skills such as ability to use tools correctly and personal qualities such as punctuality and initiative.

2. This information should be presented in a structured form (though not necessarily graded) and roughly the same kinds of information should be available for each pupil.

3. The profile report should be designed to be given to the pupils when they leave school rather than as a confidential document which is sent direct to users.

4. The profile report should be available to all pupils within the specified target group. School Certificates which were presented to particular pupils who had played a very active part in the life of the school and so 'won' them, would be excluded for the purpose of the study.

Just over a quarter of the schools that replied appeared to be offering their pupils something which more closely resembled a testimonial. Entries on these usually took the form of unstructured descriptive statements and typically included only positive attributes. Another quarter provided detailed, structured but confidential reports for the careers service, employers and further education. These were sometimes discussed with pupils but were often marked 'confidential' and forwarded directly to the user, and so could not be taken away and used by the pupil. Other schools were using a scheme based on the Record of Personal Achievement or Record of Personal Experience, which includes no teacher assessment.

Only twenty-five of the schools returning questionnaires were using a profile report which approached the criteria outlined above. Thirteen of these schools were for pupils aged 11-16, and the high proportion of such schools* presumably reflects the fact that the need to provide information for sixteen-year-old school-leavers is even greater when a whole year group leaves together. In thirteen of the schools all the staff teaching and/or tutoring fifth year pupils were involved; in five schools form tutors made the assessments. The status of the teacher in charge of the scheme varied: in four cases it was the head, in ten the deputy or senior teacher, in nine the head of fourth and/or fifth year, and in two the head of the department responsible for courses for the less able. (In eighteen schools profile reports were compulsory for all pupils within the target group whereas in seven the profile report was optional.)

Seventeen of the schools said they had developed their own profile report; six formed a local consortium and had developed a group scheme; two said they had 'borrowed' their profile report from Evesham High School. Two other schools had been influenced by the Evesham scheme. The only other influences which were mentioned by more than one school were the work of the Scottish Council for Research in Education and the Record of Personal Achievement (or Experience). The most commonly given reason for developing a profile report was that the school wanted to recognize the non-examination aspects of school life (seventeen schools); ten had wanted to make information more readily available to employers, and eight thought a profile report would help pupil motivation. Half the schools had only introduced their profile report during the academic year 1980-81 and very few schools reported changes in their curriculum or their examination entry policy as a result of its introduction.

In the belief that the compilation of profile reports is a complex process, involving many members of staff and cutting across academic/ pastoral and subject boundaries, a limited number of schools were selected for study in depth; nine were asked to take part in this second, detailed stage of the study. All agreed to co-operate. Within this small sample it was not possible to choose schools which were in any way representative of all English secondary schools, but some

---

* Only a third of all secondary schools in England were of this type. E.g. in January 1981 there were 1125 comprehensive schools for pupils aged 11-16 and 2036 for those aged 11-18. However, the LEAs claiming profile report schemes listed 107 schools for 11-16 year-olds and 110 for 11-18 year-olds that were either operating or introducing such schemes. One or two LEAs did not distinguish by age range. The present survey dealt only with schemes in operation.

attempt was made to ensure a geographic spread and to include schools of different sizes and age ranges (e.g. 11-16, 13-18). In these two respects the nine schools were more or less representative of the schools offering profile reports. A range of reports was offered by the nine but three provided a similar document, hence its operation across a number of schools in different areas could be considered (see Appendix, Table A.1).

Seven of the profile report schemes studied in depth met all the criteria described above, but the other two were chosen so that areas of particular interest could be looked at. For example, school D's profiling is based on pupil self-assessment: pupils write part of their fourth-year report and copies are used to provide information for employers before pupils take part in the school's Work Sampling scheme. School C's Leaver's Profile Report is a confidential document but the school was included because, as a member of a consortium, it gave the opportunity to look at the use of a single document across several schools. It seems likely that the schools will decide that this should be a public document in the future.

The nine schools were visited for periods varying from two to five days (except one school where all interviewing was done in one day by two researchers). Limited time made it important to see those teachers likely to have the greatest knowledge of the profile report scheme. The staff to be interviewed were specified by the researcher and schools were very helpful in making them available. In most of the schools those interviewed were the headteacher, the deputy with responsibility for the curriculum, the heads of large teaching departments (usually English and mathematics but sometimes craft and design or science as well), the heads of the fourth and fifth years (head of house in school H), the careers teacher and assistant teachers who were fifth-year tutors.

The interview lasted 40-60 minutes and was thematic, with a check-list of topics to be covered, and most were tape-recorded and trans-cribed. Where this was not feasible, details were written up immediately after the interview.

In five schools pupils took part in group discussion, but the delay in receiving the names of schools meant that some visits had to take place in the summer term when fifth-year pupils were not available. The group discussions generally lasted about forty-five minutes and again a checklist of topics to be covered was used. Some employers, careers officers and teachers in further education were interviewed but numbers were necessarily limited. This was even truer of parents: organizing interviews with them was not possible. Clearly their views are extremely important and it would be interesting to elicit these when profile reports are more firmly established in schools.

The following four chapters of this report are based on the information obtained during these interviews and group discussions. Occasionally communications from the questionnaire schools have been quoted; this is always made clear in the text.

4 THE STUDY SCHOOLS:

RATIONALE FOR PROFILE REPORTS

The wide public discussion of profile reports in the educational press
did not appear unduly to have influenced the thinking of the study
schools when they considered introducing profile reports. With one
exception the reports had been developed within the school; in-service
training through higher education courses, LEA advisers or teachers'
centres was rarely mentioned as an influential factor. In general the
schools appear to have concluded that they wanted to develop profile
reports for their school-leavers, then to have surveyed current practice
elsewhere in order to consider how this could be adapted to their
particular needs. The most salient of the reasons for introducing
profile reports were, first, curricular: a belief in recognizing the
importance of the non-examination aspects of schooling by emphasizing
the development of personal qualities and cross-curricular skills;
second, a desire to improve pupil motivation by involving students in
their assessment process or by making it clear that their behaviour and
attitude could affect their leaving statement; and third, a wish to
provide more appropriate information for employers.

Most of the schools held that the introduction of profile reports
(not just the final statement but also the process used to compile the
profile) would encourage the development of personal qualities such as
punctuality and perseverance and make it clear that schools were not
solely concerned with a pupil's ability to pass examinations. In practice, the development of profile reports seems often to have begun with
a concern for non-academic pupils:

> 'It was originally introduced as an experiment to provide something
> for those people who were going to leave the school without any
> kind of qualification.' (Deputy head)

The schools felt that these pupils, who were unlikely to achieve
more than low grades in the CSE, still had much to offer, and that
profile reports could give evidence of qualities not measured by
traditional examinations and often not explicitly valued in schools but
which were still of use in the outside world:

> 'We have a great many non-academic children and we realize that
> these children still have something to offer and that many of them
> can achieve a great deal within their own sphere.' (Head of English)

> 'The children at the bottom end of the scale may not have exam
> results but may be very helpful in other ways ... If an employer
> wanted someone who was willing and had plenty of muscle power,
> one of these boys would be ideal.' (Fifth form tutor)

There was also a fear, which appeared to be unfounded in practice, that the introduction of the single system of examining at 16+ would make it more difficult to enter pupils of below-average ability for public examinations and that a profile report would be their only 'qualification':

'I think we're looking to the future when 16+ comes in. There will be less children taking exams then and so a lot of children will be leaving school without anything at all, and this was something that all children could leave with.' (Head of department)

Nevertheless, in seven schools out of the nine, the profile reports were completed for, and available to, all pupils. This was partly on the grounds that 'If it's relevant to the less able, it's relevant to all' (year head), partly because the schools felt it would not be valued highly, either within or outside the school, if profile reports were confined to the less able and if the possession of a profile labelled a pupil 'below average'.

'Motivation' was commonly mentioned as a reason for introducing profile reports. High standards of punctuality, attendance, appearance (especially wearing uniform), conduct and attitude to learning were mentioned by various teachers as indicators of motivation; some stressed that the profile on which these qualities were recorded encouraged pupils to try and improve:

'Some of the lower ability boys were particularly interested. They saw it as something they could do and were very keen.' (Head of department)

Others suggested that the effects of the profile report were more superficial; a typical comment was:

'It does seem to motivate the lads to be on time and to attend regularly when they know it's being filled in.' (Fifth form tutor)

Many of the schools recognized that a single end-of-course profile assessment was unlikely to motivate pupils any more than an end-of-course examination. This was one of the reasons for seven of the schools involving their pupils in the assessment process. The extent of the involvement varied from school to school, and it was brought about in a number of different ways. In school D the pupils assessed themselves and the profile report was their own creation. In schools E, H and I pupils decided when they thought they had mastered a certain skill and the teacher validated a profile entry. In school G the profile was completed in the pupils' presence and they (and their parents) were asked to comment on it. In schools A and C it was intended that, after each round of teacher assessments (made two or three times a year), the results would be discussed with the pupil in the hope that poor performance would be improved. Teachers in the seven schools felt that pupil participation was a vital aspect of the profile report:

'I think the crucial part of the whole process is that the children actually sit down and are forced to think about themselves ... the actual process of thinking about it is most important.' (Fourth year tutor)

'The fact that the children are responsible for getting their ... Record filled in is part of their training.' (Senior teacher)

Eight of the nine questionnaires returned by the study schools were completed by heads or their deputies. These replies tended to emphasize the curricular and motivational reasons described above for introducing profile reports. The provision of a qualification was cited as a less important reason. Other teachers, however, were far more likely to mention the value of profile reports for employers and to suggest that this was why they were introduced into the school:

'I suppose we originally started the scheme to give our kids a better chance with employers.' (Head of careers)

'He [the headmaster] presented it in terms of the advantages it would bring in getting jobs.' (Head of department)

Additionally, some teachers expressed the fear that profile reports would be less effective as a motivator as long as the current high levels of unemployment persisted:

'I don't know how well it works as a motivator when the youngsters know there are no jobs for them to go to when they leave.' (Head of careers)

It appears that profile reports have been used in some schools in much the same way as examination results: as an inducement and as a reward for hard work and good behaviour:

'It was to be used to give kids something to work for and as a carrot: if you don't work you don't get a good profile report.' (Fifth year head)

However, the process of assessment and recording could offer the opportunity for pupils and teachers to discuss their work and to encourage students to feel that their views are valued by the school. It appeared that the profile report's main value was increasingly perceived in terms of this process for communication within the school rather than in the final public document presenting information to the employer. The opportunities that the process provides for discussion and guidance could also bring about necessary curricular changes. The lack of agreement between heads (and deputies) and other teachers over why profile reports were introduced may be the result of a change of views brought about by increased youth unemployment. Providing information for employers may have been a powerful impetus but headteachers have realized that profiles have much to contribute to pupil motivation and self-development and this has become an important rationale for profile reporting.

TYPES OF PROFILE CONTENT

Schools hoped that the information they provided in their profile report would offer a broad picture of each sixteen-year-old. The name of the document, the form in which items were entered and way in which the assessment was made varied from school to school. There was considerably more agreement over content. Table A.2 in the Appendix gives details of each school's profile report and the profile reports (or extracts from those that are too large to include in full) are reproduced as the examples in the Appendix. Reference should be made to these for detailed information on content.

There was a considerable similarity in the content of the profile reports of the nine schools, in terms of both broad areas of experience and individual items. In addition, most areas necessarily overlap.

1. Subjects studied during the fourth and fifth years

As each O-level and CSE examination generally assesses work done in a single subject area, most secondary schools organize the teaching of their fourth and fifth years according to subjects. Typically, pupils study seven or eight subjects for public examinations, and other classes such as physical education, careers and personal development are generally non-examination courses. All but one of the schools included details of the subjects studied during the fourth and fifth years. The presentation of this information varied considerably. In two of the schools the profile report included school-based assessments or certificates for each subject studied. These certificates therefore indicated the subjects studied during the fourth and fifth years as well as the standard achieved in each. Four of the schools listed the subjects studied and whether the pupils were to be entered for CSE or O-level. Two schools listed the subjects studied but did not show whether the pupil was entering for GCE or CSE examinations.

2. Estimated or 'trial' public examination results

Most schools agreed that if a profile report was to be of full use to pupils when they left school their level of academic achievement would need to be indicated. The usual way of demonstrating this to employers and institutions of further education is through examination results but these were not generally available when the profile reports were completed. This difficulty was overcome in different ways: three schools provided the results of the mock public examination which had already been taken and two schools gave teacher estimates of the grades likely to be achieved in the actual examination. Some of the schools left space on the profile report so that actual results could be entered when available.

3. Cognitive abilities

Many critics of public examinations suggest that the overall grade awarded does not give sufficient information about pupils' specific achievement or their strengths and weaknesses within a particular subject. An O-level in English language, for instance, does not necessarily demonstrate that a student is able to debate a point of view clearly or even spell accurately, and an O-level in mathematics does not always indicate accuracy in arithmetic. Employers often desire this particular information and most of the schools include assessments of basic skills such as literacy and numeracy. The range of skills assessed varies widely but tends to fall either in broad categories such as 'writing' and 'use of number' or lists of skills which break these categories up into small parts.

4. Cross-curricular skills

Profile reports could provide such detailed assessments of the student's abilities in a particular domain and also allow for assessments across the curriculum. Sometimes these skills are considered across subject boundaries and all who teach a particular pupil are asked to make an assessment of the skill when they feel the pupil can demonstrate it. However, in most schools the assessment is subject-based; for example, 'listening' is assessed by English teachers and 'use of number' by mathematics teachers.

5. Practical skills

Practical skills and abilities such as 'manual dexterity' or 'physical co-ordination' were also assessed to a greater or lesser extent in all schools. Some schools assessed broad categories; in others the categories were divided into smaller components so that students could demonstrate precise skills. For instance, the ability to select and use basic tools or understand and use working drawings would contribute to the reader's knowledge of the student's manual dexterity, and the ability to iron or to wire a three-pin plug would provide some information about physical co-ordination. Pupils could often add information about their practical abilities when they made contributions to their own profile. Entries about hobbies such as brass-rubbing, furniture restoration or motor-bike maintenance might give better proof of practical abilities than school subjects. Given the subject-based nature of the assessment, this was particularly true of those students whose course did not include a practical subject.

6. Personal qualities and social skills

Personal qualities and social skills were assessed in all profile reports. Every school included information about attendance and punctuality. Apart from these two qualities, the ability to function as a member of a group was the social skill most likely to be assessed (seven schools did so). Six schools made judgements on personal appearance and dress. The concern here was generally whether or not school uniform was worn. One form tutor said:

'Such things as tidiness of hair and clean fingernails don't really come into it.'

and another:

> 'I refused to sign for one girl because she refused to wear a tie, had blue hair and wore plimsolls.'

General behaviour, courtesy and politeness were assessed in five schools and leadership and initiative appeared in four of the profile reports. Sometimes information was provided which would enable the reader to decide whether these qualities were present: ability to receive and escort school visitors or take part in a school assembly might indicate reliability or self-confidence or politeness. (The question of assessment in this area is pursued further on pp.25-6.)

7. Interests and leisure activities

Interests and leisure activities were regularly included in the profile report: all schools provided space for pupils to give this information so that the picture given of the pupil was as detailed as possible. In one school this was restricted to school-based activities/awards so that entries could be verified easily by a teacher but most of the schools felt that it was this section which gave pupils most scope to show their individuality. Pupils did not always find it easy to provide this information. One school tried to overcome the problem by providing a reference list of possible leisure activities at the beginning of the fifth year. Staff also hoped that pupils would be encouraged to take up some of the activities during the year so that they would be able to make entries in their profile. Membership of sports teams or clubs, and participation in community service such as helping old people and baby-sitting were commonly entered by pupils. Parents, youth workers and employers were often asked to validate entries. One school further recognized the importance of the pupils' life outside school by asking parents to enter their comments.

APPEARANCE OF THE PROFILE

Profile reports come in all shapes, sizes and colours. Those from the study schools ranged from one folded sheet of A4 paper to a voluminous file weighing nearly 2 lb (900 grammes). All the schools felt that the appearance of the profile report was important if it was to have any status, and a good deal of trouble seemed to have been taken with layout and design. On the whole, cost had been kept fairly low and some schools mentioned that this had been regarded as an issue. One profile report was fairly expensive but this had been justified: when the scheme was first introduced, it was only available to lower-ability pupils and so was perceived as an alternative to entry for public examinations; the cost of the profile report was therefore compared with the costs of entry. This profile was a large blue plastic file with gold lettering on the outside and 24 plastic sleeves inside to hold subject assessments and certificates; another school's profile report had a similar format. The others were considerably slighter: one consisted of a card cover containing four A4 sheets of self-carbonating paper; other schools provided a small log book comprising eight pages inside a card cover; two schools used simple A4 sized sheets of paper or card folded in half, and in the schools where the pupils assessed themselves the three sections of the profile report were written on separate self-carbonating school report slips. Some idea of the style and layout of the profiles can be gained by looking at the examples in the Appendix.

RESPONSIBILITY FOR CONTENT AND CONTROL OF FINAL DOCUMENT

The part pupils played in producing the profile report varied considerably from school to school. In one school all the assessments were made by the staff and the pupils only saw the completed document. At the other end of the spectrum was a school where all the assessment was done by the pupils, form tutors only offering advice on request (see p.22). Between these two points came varying degrees of pupil involvement: in three schools the assessments were made by teachers and discussed (though rarely changed) with pupils. The profile in another school was filled in during form periods and so the pupils were always aware of the assessments and could write their own comments. In three schools the pupils decided when they had mastered a particular skill and then asked designated members of staff to validate the entry by signing the log book.

In most cases pupils did not have full control of the final document. One of the reasons given for introducing profile reporting was the provision of additional information about school-leavers. Requests for references are often received several years after a pupil has left the school, and so it is not surprising that four of the schools kept copies of the report and three others kept master sheets on which fifth form tutors recorded which skills had been mastered by the pupils. Schools will therefore still send out references, sometimes based on the profile, whenever they are requested by outside bodies.

*

Assessment is an integral part of content and format but for purposes of clarity it is discussed separately in the next chapter.

6 THE STUDY SCHOOLS

MAKING AND RECORDING PROFILE ASSESSMENTS

There are five major dimensions in making an assessment:

1. what is assessed;
2. who makes the assessment;
3. how the assessment is made;
4. the timing of the assessment;
5. for whom the assessment is made, i.e. the user.

The first has been discussed fairly comprehensively in Chapter 5 and the others will now be considered in greater detail. The process of recording the assessment is inextricably related to the making of the assessment and this is discussed at appropriate places in the following paragraphs.

WHO MAKES THE ASSESSMENT?

Teacher assessment

In all but one of the schools the bulk of the assessment was carried out by teachers. Generally, most staff teaching the fourth and fifth year were involved to some extent, but the brunt of the work was carried by fourth and fifth form tutors, English and mathematics teachers and, to a lesser extent, craft teachers. The number involved in assessing a specific item (e.g. 'language' or 'initiative') varied from one teacher to six or seven.

Pupil self-assessment

As indicated, most of the schools asked pupils to give details of their interests and out-of-school activities. One school asked pupils to write comments in their own profile report (these comments could provide explanations or extra information). In school D the pupils assessed themselves (see Appendix) but with the knowledge that their assessment would be read by their parents and certain members of staff. The pupils were given prompt sheets which gave examples of items which could be included in their profile report; grids were provided so that the item could be assessed on a five-point scale, ranging from 'of no importance at all, I give no time or attention to this' to 'of the greatest importance, I spend every available moment on this'. These assessments were then used to write three sections of their fourth year school report. The reports were read by the form tutor, who could advise that important information had been omitted or that insufficient detail had been included to support particular statements and suggest that this be incorporated. Some tutors corrected the spelling and grammar, others considered this was the concern of the student, but they did not appear to censor or actually make assessments themselves.

Making the assessment is only the first stage in what tends to be a very lengthy compilation process which seems to become more complex as more teachers are involved. Collation was not simply a matter of copying from a class list on to the individual's profile report. If a number of teachers had made different assessments of a particular skill, someone (usually the form tutor) had to decide on the final, global entry. Schools indicated that there was not often a major discrepancy but in one school staff were advised:

'... to translate the letters into numbers (A = 1, B = 2) add them up and then divide if they couldn't work out whether 3 Cs was worth an A and 2 Ds.' (Deputy head)

This was not always felt to be satisfactory, especially when few members of staff graded a skill, as then:

'A pupil may get an A for [physical education] and a D for woodwork. Then I enter B/C for physical co-ordination.' (Form tutor)

Thus a pupil's strengths and weaknesses could be concealed as much by the profile report as they would be by the public examination system.

There often seemed to be an informal filtering process before an entry was finally made on the profile report. It was generally recognized that members of staff were unlikely to be consistent:

'One person's assessment is different from another's. You're always going to have that problem. I'm faced with variation of standards every day of my school life.' (Headmaster)

This meant that someone (usually a senior member of staff) had to look at the grades given and decide whether the assessment should be entered on the profile report:

'I came across cases where a boy did have ability but he was a discipline problem and had been given poor grades because of this. I modified these when I came across them.' (Fifth year head)

(Consistency is discussed further under 'The user', pp.27-8)

School D tried to avoid the problems by asking one member of staff to assess each item. For instance, the form teacher would complete the entries on 'character' (sometimes after informal discussion with other members of staff), 'use of number' would be assessed by the mathematics teacher, 'physical co-ordination' by the physical education staff. This created other difficulties: first, if a pupil did not study, say, art in the fourth and fifth years, an assessment of, for example, 'visual understanding and expression' was not made. Secondly, because the judgement was made by only one member of staff it could be thought to be more idiosyncratic. A head of department in one school was typical in this respect when he commented:

'I suppose it would be a more valid judgement if it were done by four or five different people but it comes down to the time factor. They take hours to do as it is.'

Thirdly, cross-curricular skills might not be adequately assessed if this approach were adopted. For instance, 'use of number' could be assessed by science and sociology teachers as well as mathematicians.

The scheme used in three schools involved the assessment of a large number of discrete items rather than broad categories. The member of staff designated to assess a particular entry (for example, in one school the English teacher for language skills such as legible hand-writing and simple punctuation, in another the form tutor for the majority of personal qualities such as punctuality and attendance) generally signed the log book on request. Entries were then entered on record sheets and in two schools the signature had to be endorsed by a 'stamp-holder'. This endorsement was usually only a matter of form but a few instances were described where inconsistent standards had caused problems. A form tutor at one school had signed 'has been pleasant and well-mannered' for a pupil whose conduct was considered unsatisfactory by other members of staff and by the head of house. In this instance a written entry was made on the profile report indicating that this assessment only applied to behaviour in certain circumstances.

HOW THE ASSESSMENT IS MADE

Three systems of assessment can be discerned in school practice: normative, where a pupil's performance is compared with others (generally in the same year or teaching group), ipsative, where a pupil's level of achievement is compared with his/her own past performance, and criterion-referenced, where levels of performance are clearly defined in advance and pupils must show that they have reached the standard specified. In practice, teachers tended to use a mixture of these systems and did not always make their assessments in the way the teacher in charge of the profile report scheme had envisaged.

Two schools used a system based on normative assessment with a five-point scale but, whereas teachers in one of them were asked to make their comparisons 'relative to the whole age group', in the other the assessment was made relative to the small, lower ability band.* One school (B) used a four-point scale; written guidelines indicated that roughly 25% of the year group should be awarded each grade and also the nature of the performance which would merit a particular grade. An A for writing should be given when the pupil 'consistently writes material that is technically correct, lucid, fluent and logical, expression is appropriate to the task', a D would be awarded when the 'material is poorly organized, frequently irrelevant and inaccurate and, where more than a simple message is required, spelling, punctuation and grammar are poor'. Three of the schools operated what is essentially a pass/fail system: an item is signed when in the opinion of the teacher a specified level of performance has been achieved. In two of the profiles each item has a number of levels of achievement listed and an entry is made in the appropriate place.

Teachers' knowledge of their pupils, which enabled them to make their assessments, was built up over time and in many different ways. There

_____

* Now extended to the whole of years 4 and 5.

was continuing classroom observation, continuous assessment of classwork and homework and tests given during the year. Sometimes tests were given specifically for the profile report so that the mastery of a particular skill could be checked. Some of these tests were conducted informally: for example, a head of department used part of a particular section of a textbook and suggested that the members of his department did the same. Others used oral methods:

> 'When I wrote "can read and understand a popular newspaper", I didn't anticipate bringing in a popular newspaper but the most natural thing was to do so. I asked them to look at a particular article for a short time and then come along and read a bit of it, discuss it and answer questions about it.' (Head of department)

In school B some specific tests were supposed to be given to all pupils before certain items could be signed. This was not always done:

> 'I apply it religiously to the less able or middle ability range. With pupils taking O-levels I think it rather a waste of time and I just sign them.' (Assistant teacher)

School F used standardized tests (that is, tests which have been piloted on large groups so that they are applicable to a prescribed range of ability) for some of the basic skills, and these were administered to all the pupils taking part in the scheme, namely, the lower ability band. School H had introduced standardized tests in junior forms of the school and the deputy head felt that these might provide valuable information for the profile report in the future.

Teachers are continually making judgements; nevertheless some of them found assessing for the profile report, which suggests precision and formality, much more difficult. The categories on the documents were sometimes criticized as meaningless and it was said to be difficult to decide on the level of achievement required:

> '"Can write a clear and accurate report" - well, what is a clear, accurate report? What is a clear report to a ... firm where probably the gaffer himself can't spell or punctuate will not be good enough for an employer such as a newspaper. What do you mean by "accurate" - how accurate and how clear? (Head of department)

A number of teachers complained that the criteria were too discrete:

> 'The gap between "can handle routine calculations with practice" and "can barely cope with simple calculations" is too large.' (Deputy head)

and there was some criticism of the system of signing only when a skill had been mastered because there was no way of showing that a pupil had almost achieved the standard:

> 'It would be better to have some sort of five-point scale because this way does not really allow for the near-achiever — you've either got it or you haven't.' (Head of department)

There were even greater problems when it came to making judgements about personal qualities. Some teachers were unhappy about assessing these at all; a typical comment of this type was:

> 'My opinion is that teachers can make judgements on the
> academic progress of pupils but shouldn't make judgements about
> character or things like "works well with others".' (Head of
> department)

There was also the problem of definition:

> 'How honest is "honest"? Hands in a fiver, pockets a 50p?'
> (Chairman of local school working party)

and, more important, of having the evidence to make the judgement. This
was brought up frequently and some teachers felt that they were not
necessarily in a good position to make these assessments. For instance,
a deputy head believed:

> 'The majority of school programmes don't want youngsters to show
> initiative. They want complacency, doggedness and acceptance.'

The lack of consensus and detailed criteria for making judgements
about personal qualities may mean that academic attainment affects the
grades given:

> 'It's very difficult. They don't have very much opportunity to show
> initiative. The grades I give are very often linked to academic
> achievement. If I'm giving a 1 for "achievement" I'll probably
> give an A for "initiative".' (Fifth form tutor)

A fifth year head who monitored the entries on the profile report
realized this was happening and also that poor behaviour could lead to
lower grades being given for attainment. He altered grades in the light
of his own knowledge of the pupil:

> 'I think the assessment of things like initiative, potential and
> level of basic skills are in most cases inaccurate and in some cases
> sheer fabrication.'

A number of teachers thought that in practice pupils were given the
benefit of the doubt:

> 'If there isn't some evidence to the contrary the item is signed.
> In the case of "honesty" if there were concrete evidence of
> dishonesty it wouldn't be signed, otherwise it would be.' (Head-
> master)

In this context the idea of allowing pupils to choose the member of
staff who will assess personal qualities is interesting. The students
chose teachers they liked and who they thought would give good grades,
and so built on their relationship with a particular teacher who knew
them well (in theory at least) to improve their profile report.

TIMING

The profile reports covered only a limited part of a pupil's school
career. Pupils in school D were encouraged to consider what they were
like at the time of writing, that is, the summer term of their fourth

year. Three of the schools based their reports on the fourth and fifth
years and five schools concentrated on the fifth year only. Teachers
suggested that each of these arrangements caused problems. Where a
'fresh start' in the fifth year was the assessment policy, the profile
was based only on knowledge gained during that year, with the result
that:

> '... the major snag is, we start it after Christmas and it has to be
> completed by Easter, so it is really only a profile of the pupil's
> last six months at school ... there's no ongoing assessment.'
> (Deputy head)

In one of the schools which did make assessments throughout the
fourth and fifth years teachers were not in agreement about the meaning
of continuous assessment. In school I, discussion with the form tutor
after the periodic assessment was an integral part of the profile. Some
teachers hoped that the pupils would have improved their performance as
a result of counselling and that the final assessment would be best and
would appear on the report. Others believed that the termly assessments
should be averaged for the final document and so high grades in the
fourth year would cancel out any decline in the fifth year and vice
versa. This was the procedure adopted at school A.

In three of the schools pupils kept the profiles throughout their
fifth year and could give them in for signature by the headteacher and a
representative of the governors just before Easter. In most of the
others the profiles were completed just before Easter and then available
for collection by the students. In one school, pupils could collect
their reports only when they had returned all textbooks to the school
after the summer public examinations. As the profile report was not
officially available at the time of interview, it could be borrowed to
be read by the prospective employer.

THE USER

The extent to which profile reports have to be consistent depends to
some extent on how they are to be used. Pupil motivation was given as
the reason for introducing profiles more often than providing information for employers, so it was not surprising that many of the teachers
interviewed seemed to feel that maintaining consistent standards was a
'will o' the wisp' not worth chasing:

> 'I haven't thought it necessary to moderate. The members of staff
> come and collect the stamp when they want it. I don't think we
> would do it this way if it were an important thing — it's not. It's
> only local and something pleasant for the kids to carry round in
> their pockets.' (Head of department)

There was also considerable doubt about whether comparability in assessment was possible anyway:

> 'The exam. boards have spent a hundred years trying to find methods
> of assessing pupils' work. I'm not defending GCE boards but I don't
> think any individual can do what they fail to do.' (Head of depart-
> ment)

One personnel officer echoed this when he suggested it was a question of 'know your headteachers' because inconsistencies and differing standards were inevitable, and the same view was held by one deputy head, who believed:

'The employer is the only person who can standardize. He'll soon find which schools send rose-tinted documents.'

Nevertheless, if the profiles are to complement examinations and provide usable information for employers, further education and careers officers, they have to be perceived as valid and reliable and so most of the schools did take some care to ensure consistency. Discussion, either at department or at year meetings, or informally in the staff room, seemed to be the most common method of arriving at or maintaining standards; two schools (B and D) issued written guidelines and two (B and I) expected heads of departments to monitor the assessments. At school I this was formalized by making heads of department and heads of house 'stamp-holders' as described above (p.24). School C was part of a consortium of local schools and the schools jointly formed a monitoring committee to look at the way the scheme was operating.

It was generally recognized that these measures were not totally successful. One form tutor felt that the written guidelines were often ignored:

'I think the information sheets are only used by teachers who are new to the system ... The teachers just look at the pupils in terms of good, above average, average and below average.'

Teachers appeared generally to be unfamiliar with, and uncertain of, assessment procedures. Some teachers were worried in case they were too closely involved with their pupils to make valid judgements and compared their position unfavourably with that of O-level and CSE examiners. They tended to mistake the detachment of external examiners for object-ivity and to feel that their own judgements would not be as reliable or 'fair' as assessments in public examinations. The teachers who recog-nized that subjectivity was inevitable and unregrettable were exceptions:

'I'm not sure I see much wrong with subjectivity. I dislike attempts at objectivity because it is so hard to achieve.'
(Assistant teacher)

IMPLICATIONS FOR TEACHERS

The secondary school year seemed to many teachers to be one long round of assessment. One deputy head commented that the first few weeks of the autumn term were the only time when all staff could concentrate exclusively on teaching; the rest of the year was spent setting, invigilating and marking examinations. Reports, UCCA forms,* references, and the provision of information for fifth and sixth form careers interviews, all had to be fitted in at appropriate times ... and then there were the profile reports as well. In most schools these were a relatively new development (only thirteen of the twenty-five questionnaire schools had introduced them before the 1980/81 academic year) and their place in the school round was not always well defined. If staff were asked to complete them when they had just written fifth year reports or marked examination papers, profiles might well be seen as 'the straw that broke the camel's back' (head of department).

Such resentment might be exacerbated because, unlike a school report, the profile was a novel rather than a habitual aspect of school life! Its completion at the time of the survey was not taken for granted and it was not infrequently seen as duplicating other tasks such as fifth year reports or forms for the careers service:

'I think they feel the thing is an imposition. If it was part of a regular system, they wouldn't feel this.' (Deputy head)

Nor were they seen to be crucial to a teacher's professional activity:

'It's very difficult to get my staff to do these effectively and efficiently. They are not seen to be important to the work of the ... Department. Members of staff now do it with less sense of grudge than they did four years ago but they don't necessarily put any more effort into it.' (Head of department)

This last point was echoed by a headmaster who felt that he could make his staff fill in anything but 'I can't make them do it meaningfully', and by a Scale 1[†] teacher who thought, 'For the average, idle teacher

---

* Universities Central Council on Admissions application forms for university entrance.

[†] The Burnham Scale, which is used to set teachers' salaries, is divided into a number of levels, 1 being the most junior. There is also a classification that assigns schools to various numbered groups, based on size.

it's just a question of ticking boxes'.

There was little doubt that the teachers felt the completion of profiles to be extremely time-consuming. Subject staff needed time to enable the assessments to be made, and only too frequently:

'... the system ... is prone to paralysis through human failure to do what is expected.' (Headmaster, questionnaire school)

This meant that one teacher, usually the form tutor or year head, generally had to chase the progress of others until all returns were made; at this point there might still be a good deal of tedious clerical work before the document was completed. Sometimes this work was seen as interfering with other activities which staff believed to be more important:

'The teachers just have too much to cope with in the fourth and fifth year ... I would like to feel that the pressures could be relieved slightly so that I could spend more time getting to know the kids.' (Fifth form tutor)

'The profile report is a job that teachers have to do in their spare time and of course they don't enjoy doing it.' Head of department)

Critical comments and complaints about lack of time seemed to be made more often when staff were unconvinced of the value of the documents:

'It won't receive serious consideration until it is evident that it will affect a youngster's future.' (Deputy head)

Certainly, senior staff in some of the study schools realized that it was important to convince a number of teachers of the value of the profile:

'I think if things are explained to people then nobody is going to mind. You see, we want to give our children every possible benefit that we can. The staff get a kick out of the kids' achievements.' (Head of English)

Where teachers were committed to the idea they tended to make light of the amount of work involved:

'It took an awful lot of time to complete them: about three weeks, I think. It was worth the time though. The local employers value it very highly.' (Fifth form tutor)

Although pupil motivation was one of the most frequently mentioned reasons for introducing a profile report, its value was often measured by the extent to which it was favourably regarded by outside bodies. Schools were anxious to do the best for their pupils and in many of the study schools an effort had been made to involve employers. Some teachers resented the fact that they had not been involved in the development whereas the employers had:

'I think initially people showed a lack of interest in filling it in because there was no discussion or consultation before the scheme was brought in. It was discussed with employers and then foisted on us fully formed.' (Head of department)

However, most teachers seemed to feel that the extra work was worth while if it gave their students (or at least their 'worthy' students) an advantage when they left school:

'The report worked in so far as the jobs that are going are, I think, going to people who deserve them ... My belief is that it may well have helped the right people to get the few jobs that are going.' (Head of department)

and staff closely involved in profile reporting felt that employers' attitudes could be valuable in providing support and status for the scheme:

'Employment use is peripheral but it is important for status in the school.' (Head of department)

To some extent, the degree of staff involvement during the scheme's development influenced teachers' attitudes. When the idea of profile reports had been put forward by the headteacher there seemed to be some feeling that, although there was no point in opposing profile reports, staff were not going to exert themselves unduly to make them a success:

'There were a few teachers saying the head wanted it done so that we could be the first school to have it.' (Deputy head)

'There were teachers here before who were against the scheme just because the head had pushed it.' (Head of year)

Certainly, one deputy head felt that the profile had more support because it was not suggested by the head:

'Because the proposal wasn't from management there will be more commitment.'

Where staff were encouraged to help develop the profile, they appeared to accept the idea more readily. One headteacher in this position was very appreciative of his staff:

'I had no battles at all. Not in this school. That's because we have a very dedicated and very professional staff.'

Those departments which offered courses for lower ability pupils and had developed profile reports to provide school-based assessment of these courses faced other difficulties. The teachers felt themselves undervalued by the rest of the staff and believed that their status within the school affected the extent to which the idea of profiles was accepted:

'We don't have a high status in the school, don't carry much political weight and this militates against the profile report being accepted as a large part of what the school does.'
(Scale 2 teacher)

In one school the head of department had needed to be very forceful to establish the profile scheme and some other teachers felt that it was 'a smokescreen' rather than a valuable addition to school life.

The way in which profile reports had been introduced into schools varied considerably. In several schools the original idea came from the headteacher and other teachers became involved at later stages. In two schools the headteacher had decided which scheme to use and told the teachers; in others, heads of department and pastoral heads were more frequently involved in the planning stages than other teachers. Two schools were using a profile report scheme which had been produced by a committee on which such teachers from the school were represented. The profile report of two schools was developed by departments organizing fourth and fifth year courses for the less able: in one, most of the certificates related to courses taught by the department and were designed by the head of department; in the other, subject departments which provided courses for the less able had chosen to design their own certificates. Generally the profile report has been discussed at a full staff meeting but the stage at which this was done also varied. Form tutors in several schools said they knew nothing of the scheme until they were asked to explain it to their students:

> 'The first I knew of it was when I was giving the bits of paper out to the kids.' (Form tutor)

Profile reporting appeared more likely to be found in schools for pupils aged 11-16 (as stated previously, p.13, only a third of all secondary schools in England but half the twenty-five questionnaire schools were of this type), presumably because they are forced into an awareness of the importance of certification for sixteen-year-olds. When an entire year cohort is leaving, a systematic method of providing information for the next stage of education becomes particularly important.

A document which was suitable for conveying information to a number of different destinations — sixth form colleges, colleges of further education, the Youth Opportunities Programme and employment — was viewed as essential. Four of the study schools hoped that the profile report would stand on its own and take some of the pressure of reference-writing off senior staff. In one school, where pupils collated their own profile, staff said they would like to have a system:

> '... where copies are stored in the central office so that while the youngsters were still in the last stages of our fifth year and in the years immediately following, whenever any request for a reference came in, we could get the admin. staff to draw out the appropriate profile, have it photocopied and sent out with a note saying, "This is as full a representation of this youngster as we've been able to marshall, please adjust it to your requirements or draw from it what information you like."'

The school recognized that at present this would not be possible and references would still be required but for them and other schools it remained an ideal:

> 'Originally we intended that once the children had received these the school would not give any further testimonial. That has

actually gone by the board ... there are a number of important
areas of employment where they still have their own forms and
insist that they are completed.' (Deputy head)

IMPLICATIONS FOR EMPLOYERS, CAREERS OFFICERS AND FURTHER EDUCATION INSTITUTIONS

Six of the nine study schools had involved employers, to a greater or
lesser extent, in devising their profile report schemes. The study
schools possibly had closer links with employers than is common because
they were frequently in rural areas where, in the past at least, many of
the leavers entering employment would have worked locally. In school D
employers (who were also governors) sat on the 'Profiling Committee',
which met regularly. Local employers had been involved in meetings
at school E at the planning stage and some had contributed to the cost
of printing the document. In school G employers had helped to set
an annual mathematics test which formed part of the profile. On the
back of school H's profile the following statement appears:

> 'The [school H] Record of Achievement is recognised and approved
> for testimonial purposes by the following local employers ...'

The headmaster and a number of staff at school I had close links with
local industry (e.g. the headmaster was chairman of the local association for training and education) and some discussion had taken place
about the information employers would find useful. Members of the
committee which organized the scheme in which school C took part had
visited employers and discussed the proposals, and there were employer
representatives on the monitoring committee which had been set up.

In one or two of the schools it was suggested that the interest of
employers could be a double-edged sword. It was feared that their
involvement might lead to concentration on basic skills to the detriment
of other educational areas:

> 'I didn't want employers influencing it too much in the way I think
> they're sometimes tempted to do, saying "All we want is basic
> skills, nothing else matters."' (Headmaster)

Many schools reported that employers themselves were not in agreement in their attitude to profile reports. Those employers who were
more involved with schemes seem to be more convinced of their value:

> 'The employers in this area always ask to see the report if
> they know the person is coming from this school.' (Head of
> careers)

Some of the employers interviewed during this study seemed happy with
the information they receive from schools through more traditional
routes. Few of those interviewed had much experience as 'users' because
profile reports had been so recently introduced. One employer who had
several hundred applicants for craft apprenticeships had already
consulted schools about the form his own company asked them to complete.
He wanted the information he considered important on one sheet so that
it could be seen at a glance and had been irritated by one school (which
had been involved in the earlier consultation) sending its own profile
for one boy rather than completing the agreed form. Other employers

also seemed to prefer information presented in an easily assimilable way. However, it was recognized that the novelty value of profile reports could be an advantage to those school-leavers who possess them.

The extent to which companies use references varies, as does the point at which they are taken up. Schools felt that, as more people applied for each vacancy, there seemed to be a tendency to use them (like examination results) as a preliminary sift to decide whom to interview. Other firms asked for a reference to confirm impressions gained at an interview. One personnel manager was concerned that profile reports would change recruitment policy:

> 'If we read a headmaster's report on everyone who applied before selecting for interview we might not use it only to verify our own judgements.'

Some companies take up references after the employee has started work, although giving references after an appointment has been made is apparently contrary to the policy of the Secondary Heads Association:

> 'I know of some employers in the area who take youngsters on first and send for references after. They tend to base almost all their judgements on their observation of the youngster in action — which has got a lot of sense and justice about it, but they use an unfavourable school report coming through later to remove a youngster who's proved unsatisfactory at the end of three months.' (Deputy head)

Information about students is often passed on by telephone. One training manager who had been involved in early discussions over Swindon's Record of Personal Achievement said he never employed a school-leaver without speaking to the headteacher or careers teacher. A number of schools were unhappy about this comparatively casual method of trans-mitting their knowledge of students:

> 'At the moment we conduct a hilarious dishonesty, which is, on the one hand hold up the badge of examination grades and on the other hand to slip down the phone these remarks which are good or bad.' (Head of department)

They felt unable easily to resist the pressure to respond because of the possibility of prejudicing the chance of a job for one of their pupils.

Employers suggested that a profile report would be useful only if it gave more than a traditional testimonial's positive statements. They wanted a document which portrayed a pupil 'warts and all'. Schools were aware of this and it posed some problems. The most commonly mentioned was 'situation-specific behaviour': here pupils who disliked school and behaved badly could behave very differently when they left and entered employment.

> 'We do subscribe to the idea that some youngsters who don't seem to succeed with us can clearly be predicted as likely to succeed outside. Therefore we don't want to handicap them by over-representing any mistakes or misjudgements that they've made.' (Deputy head)

Some companies were aware of this difficulty; one personnel manager suggested that 'It might be the school environment which made him "very rarely co-operative"'.

In practice, most of the employers interviewed during the study were no longer recruiting school-leavers. They tended to take their young employees from work experience trainees and often seemed to 'lean over backwards' to keep someone if they had been impressed. In the areas round many of the study schools, information from schools was more likely to be used by careers officers for Youth Opportunities Programme placement than by employers. One of their difficulties was the pressure of numbers. Even if all fifth year pupils were interviewed while they were still at school, there was only a limited time for this session, perhaps half an hour; although the extra information provided by a profile report might be extremely useful it needed to be in an easily assimilable format. The careers officers at school F found that the profile report was difficult to use because it was so bulky and in practice preferred their own documentation because it was familiar. The problem was compounded because the profile was the property of the pupil and the careers officers also needed the information on their own files. This suggests that, to be useful for the Youth Opportunities Programme, the profile would have to be designed to be easily copied and read and where the content of the report has not been negotiated (that is, discussed and agreed) between pupil and teacher, the principle that a profile report should be the responsibility of the school-leaver could easily be undermined.

Many sixteen-year-old leavers go increasingly into further education and there sometimes seemed to be less co-operation between schools and FE colleges than between schools and employers. One headmaster said that, although his local college was itself involved in developing profile reports for students, the staff's attitude had been 'we don't want anything from schools'. This may in part reflect the fact that in the past schools with sixth forms and further education colleges have competed for students. They may be less of a problem now as so many young people, unable to find jobs, want to gain further qualifications. However, sometimes the pressure on places and on courses is so great that the examination results provide the selecting mechanism:

'What counts is these fine margins between the B and C over 8 or 9 subjects.' (Deputy head)

In such cases it seems likely that other documentation will be employed. Indeed, there seems to be a tendency for each stage of education to disregard information provided by the previous institution. Some further education colleges feel they are 'second chance' institutions and they offer places to as many students as possible. One vice-principal of a sixth form college, who had been closely involved in developing the profile report used by school C, believed that the information in this document was invaluable for counselling the student at the end of the first month and that it provided a useful link between the secondary and post-16 stages of education.

A difficulty for the present study was that further education admissions policy varied from department to department and from institution to institution. The attitude of employers and further education admissions tutors to profile reports may be considered further by the project on 'The Use Made of Examination Results'* which is also part of the Schools Council's fifth programme of work.

IMPLICATIONS FOR PUPILS

To some extent, at least, pupils seemed to equate profile reports with traditional school reports, and most of the pupils spoken to during the present study seemed to take for granted a teacher's right to make judgements. However, some pupils did voice misgivings. There was a feeling that, for the assessment to be equitable, as many teachers as possible should be involved:

> 'It would be awful if only one teacher commented on something and gave a low grade. Even if the rest of the profile was very good, it could stop you getting a job.' (Pupil)

> 'If a teacher has something against you then they might write something unfair in your report. I think if the report is going to be written by the form teacher then she should discuss it with all the other teachers who have you. It should be a combined comment for the overall attitude.' (Pupil)

This concern about a teacher's ability to make judgements was repeated in other schools. While pupils accepted that poor behaviour should influence their profile, they did not want sins of the far-distant past recorded and there was a feeling that a pupil's behaviour might harmfully affect academic grades.

> 'I think they just look at behaviour. If you are good and hardworking they give you good grades. If you're bad they give you bad grades whether you're good at things or not.' (Pupil)

Nor were the students sure that staff necessarily had the knowledge to complete a profile report. This was partly because the pupils felt that their schools did not encourage them to show the qualities being assessed:

> 'I don't think a teacher would know whether we've got initiative or not. We're not really allowed to show it. I think initiative here means general conduct round the school. They don't mean able to make your own decisions.' (Pupil)

Another girl suggested that her behaviour with teachers, in a classroom, was not typical:

> 'When I'm on my own like this I can talk but when I'm in a group I just sit there and shut up.' (Pupil)

The students appreciated that the public nature of profile reports could have implications for their future:

> 'Once employers know about it, you've got to show them the certificate or they'll know there's something bad in it. And you're

---

* The draft report from this study is expected before the end of 1982.

not going to get a job with a bad certificate.' (Pupil)

Some thought that this would affect their behaviour because:

'If you're suspended it goes on to the Diploma and that's not very helpful.' (Pupil)

However, others were less sure of this and felt that the disaffected were unlikely to take the threat of a poor profile report seriously:

'The sort of pupils who come late and get into fights and things, it didn't make any difference to them. They just wanted to get out of school as quickly as possible.' (Pupil)

One boy remarked:

'If I was thinking of skiving off it might stop me but on the other hand you don't remember it every minute of the day.' (Pupil)

The pupils who had assessed themselves were also unsure of the value of their profiling. They welcomed the opportunity to find out more about themselves and:

'... to tell other people what we think we're like rather than having teachers tell us what they think we're like.' (Pupil)

but some did not feel it was going to improve their chance of employment:

'If we go to college and don't get a job next year then, in another year or two, you're going to be a different person anyway so this report won't be any use.' (Pupil)

A few pupils suggested that the process would have been more successful if there had been an element of peer assessment:

'I think it would be better if a friend did it for you.' (Pupil)

Several of the pupils who took part in discussion mentioned the value of being reminded of what they were like and of their time at school. Typical comments were:

'It's good because you can look back and see how you'd changed.' (Pupil)

'We're not good at exams but when we leave school we'll have a booklet full of ourselves and our hobbies.' (Pupil)

'It tells more about you than an exam. certificate. It reminds me of when I was at school.' (Ex-pupil)

In general, pupils seemed to support profile reports and certainly it seemed likely that a favourable profile would be preserved:

'I suppose I'll keep it if it's a good one and I'll lose it if it's a bad one.' (Pupil)

Criticism of public examinations is, to some extent, implicit in an advocacy of profile reports. Many of the early supporters of profiling started from the premise that examinations were only suitable for the top 60% of the ability range at 16+ and that an alternative assessment mechanism was required for the other 40%. The idea that public examinations are an unsatisfactory means of marking the end of the period of compulsory schooling because they do not provide all the information needed for the next stage of education or for employment is another constant theme. Some educationists suggest that, if profile reports could be made to work well, they might provide a more satis-factory alternative to public examinations at sixteen. Many feel that a well thought-out profile could encourage schools to develop and assess basic skills, improve pupil motivation, provide more effective means of guidance and curriculum evaluation, and produce useful information for employers and further education.

THE TARGET GROUP OF PUPILS

Most of the study schools provided profile reports for all their school-leavers, not only for those who were taking few or no public examinations. There were two main reasons for this: first, the belief that if the profile report provided valuable information not offered through the public examination system then it should be available to all pupils; second, a desire to keep to a minimum labels such as 'non-examination' or 'profile' pupils so that the divisive effects of the present public examination system would not be reinforced or perpetuated by the introduction of profiles.

Some schools had made their profile report scheme optional: pupils might choose whether or not to participate. This is partly an organiza-tional question; if the completion of the profile report depends on the pupil asking a teacher to sign that a particular skill has been mastered then there is no way of insisting that all take part. However, such pupil autonomy was central to much early thinking which wanted to extend a major responsibility in the assessment process to the pupils.

It is possible that making a scheme optional could lead to its becoming the province of the middle ability range: the least able will not take part because they can gain so few entries; the most able will feel that, if they are staying in education to gain further qualifica-tions, the information contained in a profile report is of little relevance to them. This occurred in one of the study schools. This phenomenon rather undermined the oft-mentioned justification that profiles, unlike public examinations, would provide opportunities for a wider range of pupils to show what they could do. However, in another school where the scheme was optional, the most able had been enthusi-astic whereas the less able were more likely to choose not to take part. Of course, in all schools pupils have it in their power not to collect or make use of the profile report themselves. It seems probable that pupils who feel they are unlikely to receive a 'good' profile, because of the standard either of their work or of their behaviour, will not take up, nor use, the report.

IMPLICATIONS FOR THE CURRICULUM

The introduction of profile reporting into schools is comparatively recent. Of the twenty-five schools in England known to the Schools Council to be operating profile reports, twelve had introduced them in the academic year 1980/81 and only six had more than three years' experience. Thus, it is too soon to judge whether profile reporting will have the long-term effect on the school curriculum which its pro-ponents hope for. This expectation (cf. Raven, *Education*, *Values and Society*[6]) is that, if certain basic skills (for example, speaking and listening) and personal qualities (for example, punctuality and initiative) are formally assessed by teachers and recorded on the profile, then the school will be obliged to provide pupils with the opportunity to demonstrate their ability in these areas as well as in the traditional academic areas assessed by public examinations. Supporters of profile reports also suggest that, if these skills and qualities are formally assessed, they will be more highly valued both inside and outside school.

Six of the study schools said that the introduction of profile reports had not affected their curriculum. The only change mentioned by more than one school was the development of a 'social education course' designed, first, to encourage the development of skills such as the ability to work with others, secondly, to allow the students to show the extent to which they could organize their own work and, thirdly, to allow the form tutors to get to know their pupils better so that they could make informed assessments. Social education programmes are one way round the problem of how to assess what is included on the profile and provide a compensatory approach. A return to first principles — the definition of curricular objectives, with the means by which pupils could achieve these and their achievement be validated, is another possibility, albeit a lengthy and complex one. In practice, no school adopted this procedure. Another, more pragmatic, means is only to include on the profile report items which the school feels it can assess already. In practice, the creation of a profile tended to be a rather haphazard process and a school may only realize later how difficult it will be to assess some items.

However, to some extent it is the very breadth of the school curriculum that makes the introduction of profile reports less straight-forward. Many subject teachers were reluctant to create courses which could be divided into easily recognized, assessed and recorded individual components because they felt that such itemization might undermine broader curricular objectives such as concept formation or appreciation of literature or other cultures. It was suggested that in some subjects the specification of basic skills in, say, reading and writing might well lead to a narrower, more rigid curriculum rather than the broader, more responsive one which it is often suggested would result. If this were the case, profile reports would have a similar effect on the curriculum to that of public examinations: they would act as a straitjacket, not as a liberator.

Many of the teachers interviewed hoped that profiles would help to motivate pupils. They thought this would come about in a number of ways: first, the pupils would be involved in their own assessment and feel that their behaviour would affect their own future. Secondly, the realization that qualities such as courtesy and discipline or behaviour were being formally recorded would encourage better behaviour; thirdly, if personal, social and practical skills were assessed, all pupils would feel valued, not only those who were likely to be academically successful; fourthly the report could lead to increased communication between teacher and pupil and so to a better understanding of the other's point of view.

In practice, neither pupils nor teachers were convinced that the profile report in itself could improve motivation for long periods of time. However, it does seem likely that, if pupils feel involved in the learning and assessment process and feel that their views are genuinely welcomed, discussed and incorporated into the profile, their attitude to school and learning will improve. Certainly some teachers felt that they knew their pupils better as a result of the profile report, and where this was used as a basis for frequent discussion between form tutor and/or year head and the pupil it seemed to provide real benefits. However, such benefits are highly dependent on staff attitudes to the profile and their degree of involvement and enthusiasm.

ASSESSMENT IMPLICATIONS

The elements to be assessed

The elements of the study schools' profile reports were described in Chapter 5. Courses taken in the fourth and fifth year, cognitive skills such as 'use of spoken language' or 'reading ability', practical skills, personal qualities and interests and leisure activities were included in most of the profiles. However, there was less consensus about the desirability of making assessments within some of these areas: some teachers were less than confident about assessing skills such as 'listening' or 'ability to work independently'. There was widespread distaste for assessing personal qualities such as 'honesty', 'appearance' and 'behaviour'.

Many teachers felt that they lacked the knowledge to make cross-curricular assessments of items such as 'listening'. Their teaching was often not organized in such a way that these assessments could easily be made and they were not always sure precisely what they were supposed to be looking for. Schools commonly left the assessment of such items to particular subject teachers, for example, 'listening' would be judged by the English teacher and 'use of number' by mathematicians. In other schools the decision about whether to assess a particular item was left to individual subject teachers, who had to decide whether they had sufficient knowledge of a particular pupil to make a judgement. Both these methods seem to undermine the idea of cross-curricular assessment.

Personal qualities and social skills appear to be elements which teachers find most difficult to assess. This is partly because they have ethical objections to making judgements about, for example, a student's honesty but also because, as with cross-curricular assessment, they do not feel confident about what they are looking for or how to make the assessment. Many teachers did not feel it was part of their professional role to make judgements in these areas. Others argued that, with the increase in pastoral responsibility, teachers have taken on more and more of the work of social workers and so have made themselves liable for these judgements. Another objection is that teachers do not have the evidence on which to base their assessments. They argue that most pupils do not have the opportunity to show initiative or leadership and that it is unfair to make such judgements about all pupils. Certainly some teachers, usually the more senior, have always made such assessments when they wrote references and so profile reports have formalized and made public this assessment activity. This in itself is not necessarily an improvement: the formalizing gives added weight and credibility to the judgement.

Who is to make the assessment?

In nearly all the study schools teachers carried out the bulk of the assessment. Usually subject teachers made most of the assessments and form tutors (who were, of course, subject teachers as well) compiled the final profile. The importance of the subject teacher presumably stems from the division of fourth and fifth year courses into subjects so that most pupils are taught by a number of different people. It is through classroom teaching that most knowledge of the pupil is gained and so it is not surprising that the profile report was so dependent on the subject teachers' expertise. They were often required to judge personal qualities and social skills as well as academic attainment.

Many form tutors felt that they did not know their students sufficiently because they did not teach all the members of their form. To offset this problem, all but one of the study schools tried to ensure that a pupil had the same form tutor for at least the fourth and the fifth year. Relationships between the student and those making the assessments seem to be crucial. Teachers will not be able to make their judgements if they do not know their pupils well and pupils will not value the profile report if they do not trust their teachers. However, there does seem to be a danger of undermining relationships because of the knowledge that judgements about personal qualities will be made. The close relationship which enables the judgement to be made could be destroyed if a pupil knew that anything said could be 'taken down and used in evidence'.

Those teachers whose job was to decide on the precise entry for the final profile report also faced a difficult task. Sometimes one teacher gave a grade at variance with those of other teachers. This was often because the behaviour of the pupil in particular lessons had caused the grade to be raised or lowered. Form tutors, year heads and deputies, who were usually the teachers who decided on the final grade, then had to use their judgement and decide whether to adjust that grade.

Pupils in the study schools assumed a variety of roles in the assessment for their reports. In one school they had a major involvement but in other schools considerably less. There are many good reasons for involving pupils in their own assessment: improved motivation, the fact that they may have the best knowledge of their own strengths and weaknesses and that there are few areas where they could be considered not to have the right to make a judgement. However, some pupils who had assessed themselves were not sure that they felt confident about making such judgements public. They felt that, if their assessment were to be read by others, they needed not only to put their weaknesses in a favourable light (the tradition of the testimonial or curriculum vitae) but also to play down strengths for fear that they would not be believed or that they would be thought to be boasting. Some of the pupils favoured peer-assessment, and it would be interesting to know how much this might differ in practice from self- or teacher-assessment.

Other adults than teachers (e.g. parents, youth workers, and employers) contributed to entries in some of the profiles. There were several advantages to this: school and home were brought more closely together, the value of certain out-of-school activities was recognized and the profile report was introduced to the local community. Unfortunately, as with pupil contributions, these entries were often confined to the back sections of the profile, so that they appeared less important than teachers' entries. There may also be some difficulties over the role of parents. Some of the pupils interviewed felt that their parents would not contribute positively to the profile. Sixteen-year-olds appear not always to have close relations with their parents because their problems in establishing an adult identity are creating difficulties, and it may be that parental contributions should be at the request of the pupil rather than automatic.

The basis of the assessment

The extent to which teachers' assessments need to be standardized within and across schools depends to some extent on the intended use of the profile. If it is for the pupil, then an assessment whereby pupils' level of achievement is compared with their own past performance is probably going to be the most effective means of encouraging improvement and charting progress. On the other hand, if the information in the profile is intended for selection for employment or further education, some combination of criterion-referencing and norm-referencing (see under 'How the assessment is made', p.24) will probably be helpful because the user may want to know what a candidate can do and also to be able to compare the performance of a number of candidates. In practice, most teachers use some form of normative assessment whenever they make judgements: criteria may be laid down but they are not always acted on; teachers and others involved in assessment are accustomed to comparing pupils in order to make their judgements and so normative assessment is operating.

Where criteria were included in a profile scheme, they were often criticized as insufficiently precise. Teachers felt it was often very difficult to decide the level of achievement indicated by words such as 'good' or 'simple'. The absence of such precision increased the level of normative judgements. However, fine precision in describing criteria can lead to a sterile set of profile items, and undoubtedly there is a real tension between reflecting a creative curriculum and achieving guaranteed consistency in the making of assessments.

The problems of definition are compounded when personal qualities are being assessed. Even the meaning of 'attendance' is open to discussion and some schools enter this on the profile report as a fraction (number of half-days absent over total possible attendance) to avoid deciding what constitutes 'good' or 'excellent' attendance. Other personal qualities depend much more on the relationship between the teacher and pupil. 'Courtesy' or 'initiative', for example, may be shown on the games field but not in the classroom and vice versa. These qualities may be evident outside school but never manifested in the classroom because the pupil dislikes school. Such situation-specific behaviour makes consistent assessment of personal qualities extremely difficult within a school and impossible across the country.

When to make the assessment

None of the schools studied in detail were then compiling profile reports which covered the five final years of compulsory secondary schooling. Those that confined the process to the fifth year argued that the increased maturity of their pupils made this an appropriate time to suggest a 'fresh start'; this put all pupils on an equal footing again and made it possible for those who had not done well lower in the school to receive a 'good' report. Other schools assessed during the fourth and fifth year for the profile; in these cases the process of making and discussing the assessments was at least as important as the final document.

If profile reports are to fulfil the expectations of many educationists and encourage a broader curriculum which is responsive to society's needs, helps to motivate pupils by involving them in this assessment, and provides detailed information about each pupil, it seems likely that the process of assessment should begin in the first year and continue throughout the pupil's time in the school. This would place the profile firmly among teachers' professional responsibilities and improve, through practice, their ability to make judgements. If pupils were also involved from the beginning, they too would be able to develop the ability to look at themselves and to analyse their strengths and weaknesses in time to try to remedy these while still at school. However, it would be essential for changes and developments in pupils' abilities to be fully recognized in order that early assessments and immature efforts would not be echoed, reducing opportunities for a fresh start.

The timing of the profile's presentation was also held to be very important in the study schools: if the final document is designed for employers and further education it is needed by Easter in the fifth year at the latest and the assessments have to be made much earlier. If the main purpose is pupil motivation, then frequent assessments would be required and the report containing the final assessment need not be ready until the pupil leaves. Some schools have developed a system whereby pupils can 'borrow' their profile report if they are going for an interview during the spring term but it is not given to the pupils until they leave.

DEMANDS CREATED BY PROFILE REPORTS

Teachers feel that profiles take up a lot of their time. The assessment, checks for consistency and compilation involve many staff and are often extra tasks which have only recently been called for. The subject teachers who generally made the assessments, the form tutor who decided on the actual entry on the report, and the fifth year head who checked each one and sometimes added a testimonial were all under pressure and some were not convinced that the time spent was worth while. The more closely teachers were involved with the scheme (both its development and operation), the more likely they were to feel positive about it. There were, however, several other factors which were important in shaping their attitudes: the amount of time which seemed to be required to complete the profile, its perceived value inside and outside school and, perhaps most important, relationships within the school.

Form tutors in particular felt that they had spent a good deal of time putting the profile report together. This process was discussed in Chapter 6 but it is useful to reiterate that it was the clerical nature of the task which was often resented. Tutors realized that, because they had to exercise judgement, compilation was not a task which could be entirely delegated to office staff, even where these were available. Some felt that the time spent collating assessments could possibly be better spent. However, others welcomed the opportunity to gain extra knowledge of their pupils, especially when individual discussion with each pupil was part of the profiling process, and a number felt that the extra work was worth while because they believed the profile was valued by pupils and employers alike. Tension between teachers in some of the schools seems to have scarred attitudes to some extent. Where teachers resented the way in which the profile report was introduced, because they felt they had not been involved in its development, or if there was personal animosity towards the person whom they perceived as responsible for the document, then less care seems to have been taken over making assessments and more resentment seems to have been expressed about the extra work involved.

If teachers had more training in observation, assessment and recording, it is possible that they would feel happier about the process of profile reporting and also be more competent in these areas. Initial teacher training often includes very little about assessment and the quality of on-the-job or in-service training varies widely within departments, from school to school and from area to area. Many of the teachers interviewed for this study indicated that the only formal training in assessment they had received came from their involvement with public examinations.

The main investment in profile reports is undoubtedly teacher time. The production of the document can also be costly! Some schools mentioned that they had adopted a format for their document which would not prove too expensive; one school was spending a considerable amount of money on its report; but most felt that, although it was essential to have a well designed document which presented the information clearly, it was also necessary to keep costs low.

USERS

As already indicated, the profile report has two main audiences: first, the pupils (and to a lesser extent their parents) and, secondly, employers and further education institutions. It is unlikely that a single document can fully serve the needs of both groups. Pupils need a scheme which can be used while they are at school to diagnose their weaknesses and strengths and to act as the basis for discussion on how the pupil's performance can be improved. This requires assessments to be made for each pupil; the presentation of all the information would lead to a bulky document which could not easily be used by people outside the school.

A copy of the report was rarely sent direct to those who asked for information: it provides a source of ready information for reference writing and for completing the form from employers and colleges and tended to be used in this way. However, schools would welcome the opportunity to send a copy because of saving time and this would make it even more important that the pupils should take part in the assessment process, in order that they were not only aware of the content of the profile but had also made substantial contributions to it. Not all teachers were convinced that they should provide all this information or that it was part of their job to fit round pegs into round holes for employers. One way round this would be to have two documents: a 'formative' profile for the pupils while they are at school and a 'summative' leaving statement which provides the information which the school feels it can reliably provide for use outside.

To some extent schools have been overtaken by events. Many of the schools taking part in the present study are in areas of high unemployment and very few school-leavers are gaining jobs:* those who do often go to work for people they know. This means that in many areas the main users of profiles will be careers officers who are making placements within the Youth Opportunities Programme.

---

* For example, of school F's 1981 leavers approximately 40 had jobs out of a year group of 350.

Most previous writing on the subject of profile reports has been at the
level either of theoretical discussion and educational philosophy or of
descriptions of work undertaken by a particular institution or the
practice of a specific school. This survey, although small-scale, has
afforded opportunities to sample practices in a range of schools and to
glean something approaching a synoptic view of profile developments in
the field. It is apparent that discussion and advocacy of profile
reports have not been matched by the work undertaken by schools and thus
any conclusions as a result of such early developments must be tentative.
Certainly the field experiments currently being undertaken by the
Schools Council on 'Profiles at 16+: Support of Good Practice'* will
provide further valuable information about the implications of
introducing profile reports in schools. The two studies should be
considered together. Nevertheless, the purpose of the present survey
was to take stock of current work, to highlight issues, identify good
practice and suggest ways in which those in education might wish to
proceed. Chapter 8 explored the salient issues and this final chapter
attempts to offer some broad conclusions and recommendations of both a
general and a particular nature.

Examinations

Few schools operating profile reports appear to view them as a
substitute for public examinations but this may be a pragmatic rather
than a philosophic stance. While public examination system remains,
profiles will be viewed as a supplementary form of documentation; the
results of GCE O-level and CSE provide a preliminary sift for employers
and other users such as schools, colleges and higher education
institutions. Undoubtedly the effectiveness of a profile report as a
qualification will be undermined while the public examination system at
16+ continues. It would be a bold person who would suggest abolishing
this system; the present chapter thus accepts the inevitability of 16+
examinations continuing for the near future and further conclusions and
recommendations are made in that context.

Target group

Not all schools providing profile reports offer them to the entire age
cohort. In some cases they have been developed expressly for the less
able pupils or those least likely to be entered for public examinations.
However, such discrimination appears also to undermine the effectiveness
of the profile in terms of its status in the eyes of employers and its

---

* The draft report from this study is expected in autumn 1982.

motivational properties for pupils within the schools. Teachers in
particular feel this system to be divisive and inequitable, and the
general approach should be to extend the profile to the full ability
range rather than directing it to the less able only.

Curriculum development

It is a truism that that which is assessed assumes cachet and status
within secondary education: in order to be properly valued, any
educational objective has to be assessed and recorded. Many of the
study schools accept this rationale and have adopted profile reports in
order to underwrite abilities and qualities not readily credited through
the present examination system. Nevertheless, profiles are not in
themselves a remedy for curriculum inadequacies and schools need to
ensure that they provide full educational opportunities for areas of
particular importance to be experienced by the pupils. A profile rich
in items but parsimonious in curriculum provision is likely to be an
irritant for teachers and frustrating for pupils. Profile reports which
are merely grafted on to an existing curriculum are unlikely to be
successful; schools desirous of introducing profiles will need to
examine learning and teaching objectives in order to ensure that the
reports closely reflect these and that ample opportunities are provided
for pupils to demonstrate their abilities in the items to be included.

Profile elements

In the study schools considerable overlap was discovered in profile
content. These were described in Chapter 4. There was considerable
disquiet over the inclusion of items such as 'honesty', 'perseverance',
'punctuality'. Many teachers appreciated these were areas for which
they felt a measure of educational responsibility but they were uneasy
about formalizing this process through specific assessments. Nevertheless, it was accepted that such an assessment raised the value of these
qualities in the eyes of pupils and for some this justified the
procedure. However, such lack of consensus suggests that it would be
unwise to prescribe the sorts of content to be included in profiles. To
some extent market forces may be a major influence here; however, the
profile report needs to be developed in the light of the needs of pupils
in a particular locale, in the context of the strengths of the teaching
staff of a particular school, and within the framework of open dialogue
between pupils, parents and teachers. For this reason any blanket
recommendation is unlikely to be profitable and could possibly be
harmful. It is clear that profiles work best in schools where staff and
pupils are jointly committed to the process and the inclusion of
pejorative comments and punitive assessments is unlikely to generate
such commitment from pupils and teachers.

Consultation and participation

Staff commitment appears most likely where teachers have been fully
consulted over the initiation and construction of the profile report.
The continued provision for in-service education and training would also
appear to increase teachers' confidence in their ability to contribute
constructively to the development of the profile and thus produce a
positive response. Training in assessment and record-keeping appears
thin on the ground in most areas but, if teachers come to appreciate the
complexity of the assessment process and the potential usefulness of the

report, they are more likely to accept the extra burdens it creates.

Pupil involvement

Undoubtedly the take-up by employers and other users affords status to the profile. However, in practice the usefulness of the profile report appears to lie in its effects on pupil motivation. Where used as a basis for dialogue between pupil and teacher in order to effect more expert diagnosis, more informed guidance and more sensitive counselling, the reports appeared to boost pupil self-esteem and encourage them to feel that they had a positive role to play in their own education. Pupils have a potentially valuable part to play in the whole assessment process and this should be encouraged.

Pupil self-assessment

Self-assessment by pupils is more likely to be effective when they are introduced to the concept in their first years of secondary schooling and have continual practice in making assessments. Where pupils have collaborated in the profile assessment it is more possible to justify the inclusion of sensitive items such as social and personal skills. Schools should be able to use the information in the report to write references if the content has been negotiated between teacher and pupil and if the pupil is given the final say about the personal items to be included. Details of how assessments have been made and where the information is stored should be available to all pupils and their parents. The contexts in which the assessments are made and the possibility that the information in the profile may not be transferable should be stressed on the report.

Parents

The study was not able to explore parental attitudes or involvement in any systematic way. However, parents too may be able to make useful contributions and, if they have taken part in discussions about the assessments, they may be more likely to provide a positive response.

Assessment: teacher expertise

This appears to be an area where there is little expertise and where much confusion abounds. The bulk of teachers either expressed a lack of confidence in their ability to make assessments in an informed way or were blithely unaware of the complexity and difficulty of the process. Assessment appears to play a minimal role in initial teacher training, and in-service education and training courses dealing with assessment matters are rare. Where these are provided, they are usually aimed at the senior teaching echelons. Few LEAs have appointed advisers with particular responsibility for this area. Yet teachers are expected to make judgements, draw comparisons, evaluate progress, diagnose strengths and remedy weaknesses in their pupils' learning as part of their daily teaching routine; whether they have the appropriate expertise for making such assessments is questionable.

A considerable injection of resources is essential if the development of profile reports is to be encouraged at any local or national level. Teachers need time and training to develop the necessary assessment skills. Local initiatives should be fostered so that schools can be helped to understand the possible uses and abuses of profiles and thus arrive at the best scheme for their particular needs. Teacher training should be assisted to increase the assessment components of initial training in order to improve the education of student teachers. Schools should be helped to consider how their own administration and organization can provide opportunities for assessment of pupils and also for in-service training of teachers. Information on teaching, observation and recording strategies must be made readily available so that assessment becomes more accurate. LEAs need to set up more in-service training courses which both use outside speakers and exploit local knowledge and expertise. Staff should be encouraged to take part in these courses by provision of staff cover in schools, so that the course can take place during weekdays. LEAs should consider giving an adviser responsibility for assessment and recording within each authority. Consideration should be given to scale posts in schools for assessment so that its importance is recognized and development work encouraged.

Further work

Further work needs to be done on users' attitudes to profile reports. More information about employers' own tests, entry qualifications and forms is necessary as a background to future developments on profiles.

Overview

Profile reports are not a remedy for all curriculum inadequacies or for youth unemployment. The success of profiles appears to lie in genesis at a local and individual level where time is given to curriculum implications and educational objectives and where teaching commitment and motivation is high. In such a climate profiles appear to bring many benefits and in the light of this it would be folly to make any national prescription about the form these reports should take. However, resources should be made available so that teachers' assessment skills can be developed and their attention drawn to good practice in profile reporting. It should be recognized that time is needed for this training and that profiles need to develop gradually within schools and local areas rather than be imposed from above.

APPENDIX

Table A.1 The study schools

School	Size '80-81	Burnham group	Age range	Geog. area	Catchment	Designated intake	Pastoral organization of 4th & 5th years
A	1150	12	11-18	Home counties	Balanced urban	Comprehensive	Year head rotates from 3rd to 5th year
B	1313	11	11-18	North-west	Balanced suburban	Comprehensive	Year head rotates from 4th to 5th year
C	1000	10	11-16	Midlands	Biased urban	Comprehensive	Year head rotates from 4th to 5th year
D	913	10	11-16	East Anglia	Balanced rural	Comprehensive	Year head rotates from 4th to 5th year
E	900	11	13-18	Midlands	Biased rural	Comprehensive	Head of years 4 and 5
F	1690	13	11-18	South-west	Balanced rural	Comprehensive	Year head for 5th year
G	759	10	11-16	North-west	Balanced rural	Comprehensive	Year head for 5th year
H	610	9	11-18	North-west	Balanced rural	Comprehensive	Form tutors
I	612	9	11-16	West	Biased urban	Secondary modern	Heads of house

Table A.2 Study schools' profiles

School	Title of document (if any)	Content
A	School Diploma	Subject assessment (incl. work experience & community service). Personal assessment. Activities, interests, hobbies. Testimonial
B	Fifth Year Certificate	Subject assessment. Basic skills. School-based activities & awards. Testimonial
C	Leaver's Profile Report	Personal & social skills. Basic maths & English skills. Study skills. Health. Course followed. Overall comment
D		Interests, leisure activities. Experiences of work, character, personal qualities
E	Personal Achievement Record	Course followed. Language, maths, practical, personal & social skills. Personal achievements
F	School Diploma & File of Personal Achievement	Subject assessment (incl. work experience & community service). Personal assessment. Achievements & experience. Examples of own work. Certificates. Testimonial.
G	School Leaving Report	Basic skills, character, health. Course followed. Teacher, pupil & parent comment

Form of entries	Who makes the assessment	Period of assessment	Target group	Extent of pupil control of final document
Grading on 5-point scale. Descriptive statements	Staff	Years 4 & 5	Non-exam. group in years 4, 5	Property of pupil on leaving
Grading on 4-point scale. Descriptive statements	Staff	Year 5	All pupils	Cert. given to pupil on leaving. School keeps copy
Assessment of competence. Descriptive statements	Staff	Years 4 & 5	All pupils	Report given to pupil. School keeps copy
Descriptive statements	Pupil	Mainly summer term, year 4	All pupils	Written by pupil. School keeps copy
Assessment of competence	Entries initiated by pupil, validated by staff	Year 5	Optional for all pupils	Log book belongs to pupil. School keeps record sheet
Grading on 5-point scale. Descriptive statements	Staff teaching years 4 & 5	Years 4 & 5	Optional for lower band (c. 40%) õf years 4, 5*	Property of pupil on leaving
Assessment of competence. Descriptive statements	Staff	Year 5	All pupils	Top copy given to pupil. School keeps bottom copy

(cont.)

---

* Available from September 1982 to the whole of years 4 and 5.

Table A.2 (cont.)

School	Title of document (if any)	Content
H	Record of Achievement	Course followed. Social & personal qualities & skills. English, maths, science, practical & creative skills. Personal achievements. Work experience, community service
I	Personal Achievement Record	Course followed. Practical, personal & social, language & maths skills. Personal achievements

Form of entries	Who makes the assessment	Period of assessment	Target group	Extent of pupil control of final document
Assessment of competence	Entries initiated by pupil, validated by staff	Year 5	Optional for all pupils	Log book belongs to pupil. School keeps record sheet
Assessment of competence	Entries initiated by pupil, validated by staff	Year 5	Optional for all pupils	Log book belongs to pupil. School keeps record sheet

Example 1 From school A (originally 1 A4 side).

PERSONAL ASSESSMENT

NAME_____

Qualities	Average Termly Grades						Ave.
	Autumn	Spring	Summer	Autumn	Spring		
Standard of work presentation							
Perseverance in completing a task							
Making most of his/her ability							
Ability to work without supervision							
Ability to contribute sensibly to a discussion							
Initiative							
Adaptability to new situations							
General behaviour							
Cooperation with staff and other adults							
Reliability in out-of-school visits							
Reliability in school							
Ability to form good relationships							
Maturity							
Use of leisure							
Attendance							
Punctuality							
Personal appearance and grooming							

Assessment Period _____

Personal Assessment
1. Very good
2. Good
3. Average
4. Poor
5. Very poor

Example 2 From school A (originally 2 A4 sides): front only shown. On
          reverse, 3 more termly assessment tables, finally the
          signatures of teacher and head of department.

CERTIFICATE
in
ENGLISH

TERM _____

Skills	Effort Grade	Comment
Reading		
Comprehension		
Sentence Construction		
Punctuation		
Spelling		
Essay		
Handwriting		
Verbal Skills		
Literature		

TERM _____

Skills	Effort Grade	Comment
Reading		
Comprehension		
Sentence Construction		
Punctuation		
Spelling		
Essay		
Handwriting		
Verbal Skills		
Literature		

Example 3 From school A (originally 2 A4 sides).

CERTIFICATE

in

TECHNICAL STUDIES

PERSONAL ASSESSMENT

Metalwork

	TERM				
	1	2	3	4	5
NAME					
PERSONAL QUALITIES					
IMAGINATION					
INITIATIVE					
BEHAVIOUR					
PERSEVERANCE					
ABILITY TO WORK WITH OTHERS					
RESPONSIBILITY					
SKILLS DEVELOPMENT					
USE OF MATERIALS					
USE OF TOOLS					
USE OF APPLIANCES					
USE OF MACHINE TOOLS					
REGARD FOR SAFETY					
ABILITY TO SOLVE PROBLEMS					

GRADING: | EXCELLENT| A, GOOD| B, AVERAGE C, FAIR D, POOR E

[i]

Example 3 (cont.)

Summary

TEACHER _____

HEAD OF DEPARTMENT _____

[ii]

59

Example 4 From school B (originally A4 sheet folded to make 4 pp): for convenience, p.(iv) is shown to left of p.(i).

FIFTH YEAR CERTIFICATE

19

Presented to

Name

Form

Date of birth

This is a school report based on assessments by all the teachers of this pupil.

Headmaster's Signature

[i]

TESTIMONIAL

Attendance

Punctuality

Appearance

Comment

Year Master's Signature

Requests for confidential reference should be directed to the Fifth Form Year Master at the School.

[iv]

Example 4 (cont.)

SUBJECT ASSESSMENT

The grades **1** to **4** represent subject teachers' estimates of potential, not the results of an external examination. Grade **1** refers to pupils capable of a good 'O' level pass. Grade **4** refers to pupils of non-examination standard at C.S.E.

The grades **A** to **D** represent in each case approximately one quarter of the pupils in the year group, i.e. Grade A = top 25%

SUBJECT	POTENTIAL ACHIEVEMENT	INITIATIVE	EFFORT
ENGLISH LANGUAGE			
MATHEMATICS			
PHYSICAL EDUCATION			

[ii]

LEVEL OF BASIC SKILLS

The grades **A** to **D** represent in each case approximately one quarter of the pupils in the year group.

Reading ☐

Writing ☐

Listening ☐

Speaking ☐

Additional Skills ☐ ☐ ☐
_____
_____
_____

Numeracy ☐

Manual Dexterity ☐

Visual Comprehension ☐

Physical Co-ordination ☐

SCHOOL BASED ACTIVITIES/AWARDS

Signature of Form Teacher.

[iii]

Example 5   From school C (originally A4 sheet folded to make 4 pp, 3 occupied).

LEAVER'S PROFILE REPORT

NAME	
SCHOOL	
DATE	

THIS CONFIDENTIAL REPORT IS BASED ON THE SCHOOL'S KNOWLEDGE OF THE STUDENT NAMED ABOVE. IT HAS BEEN PRODUCED AS A RESULT OF CONTINUOUS ASSESSMENT AND THE COMMENTS MADE ARE VALID UP TO THE DATE OF THE CERTIFICATE.

. . . . .Compiler   . . . . .Headteacher

[i]

Example 5   (cont.)

PUNCTUALITY		
1.		Can always be relied upon to arrive on time.
2.		Can be relied upon to arrive on time for most occasions.
3.		Cannot be relied upon to arrive on time.

ATTENDANCE		
1.		Completely satisfactory
2.		Some record of absence.
3.		Significant absences from school.

RELIABILITY		
1.		Always reliable.
2.		Normally reliable.
3.		Unreliable.

PERSEVERANCE		
1.		Usually undeterred by difficulties.
2.		Conscientious in approach to a problem.
3.		Makes reasonable efforts to overcome difficulties.
4.		Will make some effort if frequently encouraged.
5.		Rarely makes an effort.

USE OF NUMBER		
1.		Quick and accurate.
2.		Can handle routine calculations with practice.
3.		Can barely cope with simple calculations.

USE OF SPOKEN LANGUAGE		
1.		Speaks clearly and confidently with good vocabulary.
2.		Capable of reasonable expression with minimum of hesitation.
3.		Finds difficulty in speaking in complete sentences, hesitates and has limited vocabulary.

UNDERSTANDING OF SPEECH		
1.		Understands complex discussion and instructions.
2.		Understands most discussion and instructions.
3.		Has difficulty in understanding discussion and instructions often need repeating.

INITIATIVE		
1.		Shows clear initiative in most situations.
2.		Shows clear initiative if given a little guidance.
3.		Works along defined guidelines with prompting.
4.		Needs regular guidance.
5.		No initiative and needs constant guidance to continue work.

ABILITY TO WORK WITH OTHERS		
1.		Makes full contribution and takes leadership role.
2.		Makes full contribution with high level co-operation.
3.		Prefers to be directed by others but works well.
4.		Cannot always be relied upon to co-operate.
5.		Very rarely co-operative.

READING ABILITY		
1.		Can understand complex written material.
2.		Can understand all everyday written material.
3.		Limited understanding of simple material.

WRITING		
1.		Writes accurately and lucidly.
2.		Competent with everyday spelling and grammar.
3.		Experiences difficulty with most aspects of written work.

ARTISTIC/CREATIVE		
1.		Capable of understanding appropriate concepts and uses materials sympathetically.
2.		Produces sound work but may need help with new challenges or concepts.
3.		Needs constant assistance.

MANUAL DEXTERITY		
1.		Highly skilled in use of hands.
2.		Skill level satisfactory.
3.		Has limited powers of dexterity.

[ii]

Example 5   (cont.)

CURRICULUM KNOWLEDGE AND INTEREST
Subjects
and Level with grade

	Est	Act		Est	Act		Est	Act		Est	Act
	Est	Act	1.			2.			3.		
4.			5.			6.			7.		
8.			9.			10.			11.		

HEALTH AND GENERAL FITNESS

OVERALL COMMENTS

[iii]

PERSONAL PROFILE SUMMARY

NAME ....   FORM ....

My interests and leisure activities

I spend a lot of time with my family especially at weekends and when they go out. I do not spend so much time with my school friends out of school except for sports. I like playing tennis and I am in the school team. I also like cycling of which I do a lot with my brother in the immediate district. I sometimes play hockey in the school team but I do not really enjoy it. My relaxation usually involves either tennis, cycling or reading, which I greatly enjoy. I help my family quite a lot and sometimes my next door neighbours who are OAPs with gardening. This I also enjoy. My hobbies include cactus growing (I am a junior member of the National Cactus and Succulent Society) and stamp collecting. I spend some of my free time on these when I feel in the mood. I also like walking long distances across country (not on roads). I enjoyed the Peak District trip due to this. I liked being with my friends during that as I think it added to the enjoyment. Swimming is another sport I like but I am not very good.

My experiences of work

I prefer mental work involving numbers than almost anything else. I enjoy maths and the mathematical side of physics and chemistry. I enjoy all the sciences because I think they are interesting and relevant to what I will probably do for a living. I am thinking of training to be a doctor which also involves hard physical work. I like this in the form of grasscutting, tennis, cycling, some hockey, housework and swimming. My mechanical skills are not very good, neither do I really enjoy that sort of thing. I quite like creating things such as in art, but again I am not very good. I need to be given one or several ideas before I can start. Most of my work involves reading and writing and listening how to do something before I start. I do not really enjoy planning or organising for large groups, but I usually plan ahead for myself.

My character, personal qualities

I am usually a quiet person, both at home and at school, but if I say something which I think is right I will argue my point. I am quite active when the weather is nice to be out in, in the way of sports. I am careful both in what I do and what I say so that I do not upset anybody. I try not to take large unnecessary risks which put either me or anyone else into danger. I am not a good leader and I do not really like being a leader in social circles but I think many people follow (or try to follow) my example in academic subjects such as maths. I try to be co-operative to everybody if they ask me to do something which I think it is possible for me to do but I do not really like joining in large groups. I always persist in finishing everything it is possible for me to do. I attach quite a lot of importance to appearance and try always to be clean and neat, though not always fashionable. I always try to be reliable and never late unless I can help it. I always keep my word, especially where I am asked to keep a promise.

Example 7 From school E (originally 8 pp booklet in cover, 9 × 17 cm)

Personal Achievement Record

NAME OF STUDENT...

DATE OF BIRTH............................

DATE OF LEAVING..............................

[cover]

COURSE FOLLOWED

The following subjects have been studied during the last two years, at the levels shown

SUBJECTS	LEVEL	TRIAL EXAM RESULT	STAMP

Date ....

Form Tutor ....

[i]

66

Example 7 (cont.)

LANGUAGE SKILLS

	STAFF	STAMP
1. Has legible handwriting		
2. Can write simple sentences		
3. Can read and understand a popular newspaper		
4. Can use simple punctuation correctly		
5. Avoids elementary spelling mistakes		
6. Can write a personal letter		
7. Can give and take a telephone message		
8. Can accurately complete a passport application		
9. Regularly borrows from school or public library		
10. Can write a business letter		
11. Can make an accurate written report		
12. Can make a clear spoken report		
13. Can summarise accurately a notice or report		
14. Can understand simple instructions in a foreign language		
15. Can give simple instructions in a foreign language		

[ii]

MATHS SKILLS

	STAFF	STAMP
1. Has a good understanding of the rules of number		
2. Has a good accuracy in handling numbers		
3. Can apply the four rules to money with accuracy		
4. Capable of performing everyday calculations in money with accuracy		
5. Understands money transactions such as wages and income tax		
6. Able to handle decimals met in everyday life		
7. Able to handle fractions met in everyday life		
8. Understand simple percentages		
9. Understands simple profit and loss		
10. Understands metric system of measure		
11. Understands English measures of length, weight & capacity		
12. Can measure accurately		
13. Is able to use a calculator		
14. Has an understanding of V.A.T.		
15. Can read and understand time tables, wage tables and ready reckoner		

[iii]

Example 7 (cont.)

PRACTICAL SKILLS

	STAFF STAMP
1. Is aware of safety precautions in the home	
2. Is aware of safety precautions in the workshop	
3. Is aware of safety precautions in the laboratory	
4. Can select and use appropriate hand tools	
5. Can use correctly a domestic washing machine	
6. Can use correctly a domestic sewing machine	
7. Can iron correctly a shirt or dress	
8. Can understand a working drawing or pattern	
9. Can modify a working drawing or pattern	
10. Can make 3 simple joints in wood or metal	
11. Is competent in basic cookery	
12. Can choose and follow a route or a map	
13. Can express ideas in sketch or diagram form	
14. Understands scientific terms in common use	
15. Understands technical terms in common use	

[iv]

PERSONAL AND SOCIAL SKILLS

	STAFF STAMP
1. Is normally and cleanly dressed for school	
2. Is normally punctual	
3. Has a good attendance record	
4. Takes a pride in his/her work	
5. Can work well without close supervision	
6. Can work well as a member of a group	
7. Can organise his/her work efficiently	
8. Has played for a school team	
9. Can swim 25m	
10. Is a regular member of a school club or society	
11. Has attended a school residential course or expedition	
12. Can receive and escort school visitors	
13. Has taken part in school or year assemblies	
14. Has had a position of responsibility at school	
15. Shows a capacity for organisation and leadership	

[v]

Example 7 (cont)

PERSONAL ACHIEVEMENTS

ACHIEVEMENT	DATE	STAFF Signature
(The student may enter here brief details of non-scholastic achievements, both in and out of school)		

[vi]

PERSONAL ACHIEVEMENTS (Continued)

ACHIEVEMENT	DATE	STAFF Signature

[vii]

Example 7   (cont.)

This Personal Achievement Record is

Certified and approved by

....
                    Headmaster

....
                Chairman of Governors

....
                    Date

[viii]

70

Example 8 From school F (originally 2 A4 sides).

DIPLOMA FILE ASSESSMENT

STANDARDISED TESTS

BASIC SKILLS	TERM 1	2	3	4	5	COMMENT 1
1. LANGUAGE						
10 .1 VOCABULARY		☐			☐	
30 .2 COMPREHENSION	☐			☐		
10 .3 SPELLING		☐			☐	
10 .4 GRAMMAR			☐			
2. MATHEMATICS						
20 .1 CONCEPTS	☐		☐			
20 .2 PROBLEM SOLVING		☐		☐		
3. PRESENTATION						
20 .1 SPOKEN			☐		☐	
10 .2 WRITTEN		☐			☐	

4. PERSONAL SKILLS
(Referee's marks)

10 .1 PUNCTUALITY					
10 .2 COURTESY					
10 .3 EFFORT					
10 .4 BEHAVIOUR					
10 .5 HELPFULNESS					
TOTAL (100)					
ATTENDANCE %					
ASSESSMENT (100)					

5. SUBJECT ASSESSMENTS
(Interim and Final)

	4th	5th
30 .1		
30 .2		
30 .3		
30 .4		
30 .5		
50 .6 ENGLISH		
50 .7 MATHS		

COMMENT 1

2

3

DIPLOMA GRADE ☐

SUBJECT TOTAL	_____	*500	☐☐☐
SECTIONS 1-4	_____	*500	☐☐☐
Discretionary Award		(100)	☐☐☐
FINAL TOTAL		~1.000	☐☐☐

[i]

Example 8 (cont.)

PERSONAL PROFILE ☐

	4	5
REFEREE		
FORM TUTOR		
ENGLISH		
MATHS		

D.O.B. ☐☐☐

Notes:- _____
_____
_____
_____
_____

Test Results	PS	1	3	
1. Cog. Abl.				
VB				
QB				
2. Wide Span				
R/A				
3. IQ				

4. Richmond BS	PR L			
Vocab.				
Reading comp.				
Spelling				
Capitals				
Punctuation				
Usage				
(Grammar)				
5. Maths Concepts				
Problem solving				
6.				

NOTES _____
_____
_____

FILE Received _____
Placement _____

conversions

Gr	PR	10	20	30
A	90	% (PR)		
B	66			
C	23			
D	9			
E	1			

Example 9 From school F (originally 2 A4 sides).

COURSE CERTIFICATE
ENGLISH

See overleaf for:
COURSE ACHIEVEMENT PROFILE

ASSESSMENT
(relative to whole age group)

Distribution % 1o 2o 4o 2o 1o

	A	B	C	D	E
APTITUDE					
EFFORT					
ATTITUDE					
READING SKILLS					
WRITING SKILLS					
ORAL SKILLS					
ATTENDANCE					

Assessment period [   ] ~ [   ]

Teacher's Comment ~

EXAMINATION ENTRY [   ]

[i]

Example 9   (cont.)

Course Achievement Profile

Reading Skills	Grade
1. 1. Comprehension	
2. Fluency	
3. Alphabetical Skills	
4. Gathering Information	
5. Using a Library	
6. Reading to others	

Understanding	Grade
2. 7. Written Instruction	
8. Tables & Timetables	
9. Telephone Directories	
10. Newspapers	
11. Abbreviations	
12. Graphs & Diagrams	
13. Maps	
14. Formal Correspondence	
15.	
16.	

Writing Skills	Grade
3. 1. Handwriting	
2. Sentence Construction	
3. Punctuation	
4. Spelling	
5. Presentation & Planning	
6. Letter Writing	
7. Descriptive Writing	
8. Form Filling	
9. Creative Writing	
10. Notes & Lists	

Oral and Aural Skills	Grade
4. 1. Speech	
2. Discussion	
3. Telephone (use of)	
4. Relating Information	
5. Listening	

Notes

_____
_____
_____
_____
_____
_____
_____
_____

EXPLANATION OF GRADES

A awarded to 10% of age group
B awarded to 20% of age group
C awarded to 40% of age group
D awarded to 20% of age group
E awarded to 10% of age group

Overall Grade ☐

Tutor_____

Example 10 From school F (originally 1 A4 side).

DIPLOMA

PERSONAL ASSESSMENT

ASSESSMENT RELATIVE TO WHOLE AGE GROUP

	A	B	C	D	E
APPEARANCE & BEARING					
ABILITY TO COMMUNICATE					
PUNCTUALITY					
RELIABILITY					
COURTESY					
CONCERN FOR OTHERS					
PERSEVERANCE					
WORKING WITH OTHERS					
WORKING ALONE					
CURIOSITY					
INITIATIVE					
SELF CONFIDENCE					
SOCIABILITY					

THESE ASSESSMENTS ARE COMPILED BY PUPIL AND TUTOR

TUTOR _____   DATE _____

Example 11 From school G (originally 4pp A4 booklet in cover).

SCHOOL LEAVING REPORT

THIS IS A BRIEF REPORT ON...

DATE OF BIRTH   ....

YEAR OF LEAVING   ....

This Report is the result of continuous assessment by all teachers of this pupil and has the authority of:-

....
HEADTEACHER

[1]

Example 11 (cont.)

S K I L L S

LISTENING

ACTS INDEPENDENTLY AND INTELLIGENTLY ON COMPLEX VERBAL INSTRUCTIONS ☐

CAN INTERPRET AND ACT ON MOST COMPLEX INSTRUCTIONS ☐

CAN INTERPRET AND ACT ON STRAIGHTFORWARD INSTRUCTIONS ☐

CAN CARRY OUT SIMPLE INSTRUCTIONS WITH SUPERVISION ☐

FINDS DIFFICULTY ☐

SPEAKING

CAN DEBATE A POINT OF VIEW ☐

CAN MAKE A CLEAR AND ACCURATE ORAL REPORT ☐

CAN DESCRIBE EVENTS ORALLY ☐

CAN COMMUNICATE ADEQUATELY AT CONVERSATION LEVEL ☐

FINDS DIFFICULTY ☐

READING

UNDERSTANDS ALL APPROPRIATE WRITTEN MATERIAL ☐

UNDERSTANDS THE CONTENT AND IMPLICATIONS OF MOST WRITING IF SIMPLY EXPRESSED ☐

UNDERSTANDS UNCOMPLICATED IDEAS EXPRESSED IN SIMPLE LANGUAGE ☐

CAN READ MOST EVERYDAY INFORMATION SUCH AS NOTICES OR SIMPLE INSTRUCTIONS ☐

FINDS DIFFICULTY ☐

WRITING

CAN ARGUE A POINT OF VIEW IN WRITING ☐

CAN WRITE A CLEAR AND ACCURATE REPORT ☐

CAN WRITE A SIMPLE ACCOUNT OR LETTER ☐

CAN WRITE SIMPLE MESSAGES OR INSTRUCTIONS ☐

FINDS DIFFICULTY ☐

VISUAL UNDERSTANDING AND EXPRESSION

CAN COMMUNICATE COMPLEX VISUAL CONCEPTS READILY AND ACCURATELY ☐

CAN GIVE A CLEAR EXPLANATION BY SKETCHES AND DIAGRAMS ☐

CAN INTERPRET A VARIETY OF VISUAL DISPLAYS SUCH AS GRAPHS OR TRAIN TIMETABLES ☐

CAN INTERPRET SINGLE VISUAL DISPLAYS SUCH AS ROAD SIGNS OR OUTLINE MAPS ☐

FINDS DIFFICULTY ☐

USE OF NUMBERS

QUICK AND ACCURATE IN COMPLICATED OR UNFAMILIAR CALCULATIONS ☐

CAN DO FAMILIAR OR STRAIGHTFORWARD CALCULATIONS, MORE SLOWLY IF COMPLEX ☐

CAN HANDLE ROUTINE CALCULATIONS WITH PRACTICE ☐

CAN DO SIMPLE WHOLE NUMBER CALCULATIONS SUCH AS GIVING CHANGE ☐

FINDS DIFFICULTY ☐

PHYSICAL CO-ORDINATION

A NATURAL FLAIR FOR COMPLEX TASKS ☐

MASTERY OF A WIDE VARIETY OF MOVEMENTS ☐

CAN PERFORM SATISFACTORILY MOST EVERYDAY MOVEMENTS ☐

CAN PERFORM SINGLE PHYSICAL SKILLS SUCH AS LIFTING OR CLIMBING ☐

FINDS DIFFICULTY ☐

MANUAL DEXTERITY

HAS FINE CONTROL OF COMPLEX TOOLS AND EQUIPMENT ☐

SATISFACTORY USE OF MOST TOOLS AND EQUIPMENT ☐

CAN ACHIEVE SIMPLE TASKS SUCH AS WIRING A PLUG ☐

CAN USE SIMPLE TOOLS, INSTRUMENTS AND MACHINES SUCH AS A SCREW DRIVER ☐

FINDS DIFFICULTY ☐

2

Example 11 (cont.)

C H A R A C T E R

RELATIONSHIP WITH FELLOW PUPILS

A LEADER/ A DOMINANT PERSONALITY ☐

ACCEPTED MEMBER OF
  PUPIL GROUPS ☐

LIKES TO JOIN WITH OTHER PUPILS, A
  FOLLOWER ☐

      INDEPENDENT
RATHER ISOLATED, TENDS TO BE ON OWN ☐

ABILITY TO WORK WITH OTHERS

WORKS WELL AS THE LEADER OF A TEAM ☐

WORKS WELL AS A MEMBER OF A TEAM ☐

PREFERS TO WORK ON OWN ☐

DOES NOT FIT WELL AS A MEMBER OF A
TEAM ☐

ABILITY TO PROFIT FROM FURTHER TRAINING OR EDUCATION

SHOULD HAVE FURTHER TRAINING OR EDUCATION
FROM WHICH MUCH BENEFIT WOULD COME ☐

WOULD FOLLOW AN APPROPRIATE COURSE OF
  FURTHER TRAINING OR EDUCATION TO
  ADVANTAGE ☐

FURTHER TRAINING OR EDUCATION PROBABLY
NOT APPROPRIATE ☐

DISCIPLINE

SELF-DISCIPLINED - ABLE TO RELATE TO A
  NORMAL ADULT/CHILD, TEACHER/PUPIL
  SITUATION ☐

ACCEPTS A SPECIFIED PATTERN OF
  BEHAVIOUR AND RULES ☐

ACCEPTS AN IMPOSED PATTERN OF BEHAVIOUR
  AND RULES WHERE THERE IS A DEGREE OF
  SUPERVISION ☐

DOES NOT ALWAYS ACCEPT A PATTERN OF
  BEHAVIOUR REQUIRED FROM THE PUPIL
  GROUP ☐

ATTENDANCE AND PUNCTUALITY

ATTENDANCE IN THE LAST YEAR OF SCHOOL

    HALF DAYS - POSSIBLE . . . .

        ACTUAL   . . . .

PUNCTUALITY IN LAST YEAR OF SCHOOL
      EXCELLENT ☐
      SOME LATENESS ☐
      POOR ☐

NOTE HERE ANY MEDICAL REASON THAT
  HAS CAUSED MAJOR ABSENCE

HEALTH

NORMAL HEALTH THAT HAS NOT INTERFERED
  WITH SCHOOLING ☐

HAS HAD A PARTICULAR PROBLEM WITH
  HEALTH OF WHICH THE SCHOOL HAS
  HAD TO BE AWARE ☐

3

Example 11 (cont.)

SUBJECT AND ACTIVITY				
ASSESSMENT				
CURRICULUM AREA	SUBJECTS STUDIED	YEARS DURING WHICH SUBJECT STUDIED	EXAMINATIONS	
			ENTRY	FORECAST GRADE
MATHEMATICS	MATHEMATICS			
	ARITHMETIC			
	MONEY MANAGEMENT			
	COMPUTER STUDIES			
	STATISTICS			
ENGLISH LANGUAGE AND LITERATURE	ENGLISH LANGUAGE			
	ENGLISH LITERATURE			
MODERN AND CLASSICAL LANGUAGES	FRENCH			
	GERMAN			
	SPANISH			
	LATIN			
	EUROPEAN STUDIES			
PHYSICAL SCIENCES	PHYSICS			
	CHEMISTRY			
	BIOLOGY			
	BASIC SCIENCE			
	GEOLOGY			
HUMAN SCIENCES	HISTORY			
	GEOGRAPHY			
	ECONOMICS			
	SOCIOLOGY			
	CHILDWALL			
	RELIGION			
AESTHETIC AND CREATIVE SUBJECTS	ART			
	DESIGN			
	DRAMA			
	MUSIC			
	WOODWORK			
	METALWORK			
	HOUSECRAFT			
	NEEDLEWORK			
APPLIED SUBJECTS	TECHNICAL DRAWING			
	ENGINEERING SCIENCE			
	TYPEWRITING			
	RURAL SCIENCE			
	OFFICE PRACTICE			
PHYSICAL AND OUTDOOR ACTIVITIES	P.E.			
	GAMES			

4

Example 11   (cont.)

FURTHER INFORMATION AND COMMENTS

THIS SECTION OF THE REPORT IS AVAILABLE FOR THE SCHOOL, PUPIL AND PARENTS TO INCLUDE ANY OTHER
INFORMATION THAT WILL HELP TO PRESENT A TRUE AND ACCURATE PICTURE.   THIS IS WHERE INFORMATION
ABOUT SPECIAL COURSES ATTENDED, PREVIOUS SCHOOLS, HONOURS ACHIEVED ETC. CAN BE RECORDED.

ADDITIONAL SCHOOL INFORMATION

INFORMATION PROVIDED BY THE PUPIL

INFORMATION PROVIDED BY THE PARENTS

5

Example 12   From school H (originally 8 pp A5 booklet
              in cover): for convenience, cover back
              (= cover p.iv) is shown to left of cover
              front (= cover p.i).

RECORD OF ACHIEVEMENT

Name _____

[cover, i]

The School H Record of Achievement is recog-
nised and approved for testimonial purposes
by the following local employers:

Allard Exclusive Knitwear & Co. Ltd.

Allisons of Pocklington Ltd.

Armstrong-Massey Motor Engineers.

Barclays Bank Ltd.

British Aerospace.

Collings & Son Ltd., North Newbald.

Europower Hydraulics Ltd.

K. Freeman Ltd., North Newbald.

Hull & East Riding Co-operative Society Ltd.

Lloyds Bank Ltd.

Massey International Coachbuilders Ltd.

Midland Bank Ltd.

R.B.M. Agriculture.

Frank Scaife (Manorline) Ltd.

Shiptonthorpe Garage.

Stag Caravan Company Ltd., Pocklington.

J.R. Tyson (Holme) Ltd.

United Carriers, Howden.

Union Carbides (U.K.) Ltd., North Newbald.

Ernest Waters, Printer.

[cover, iv]

Example 12   (cont.)

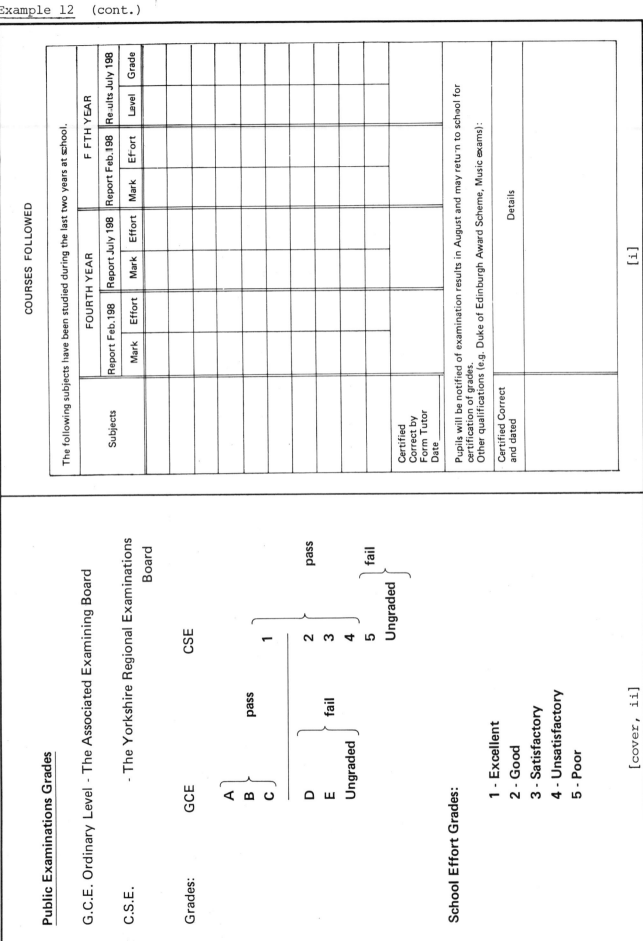

COURSES FOLLOWED

The following subjects have been studied during the last two years at school.

| Subjects | FOURTH YEAR | | | | FIFTH YEAR | | | |
| | Report Feb.198 | | Report July 198 | | Report Feb.198 | | Results July 198 | |
	Mark	Effort	Mark	Effort	Mark	Effort	Level	Grade

Certified
Correct by
Form Tutor
Date

Pupils will be notified of examination results in August and may return to school for certification of grades.
Other qualifications (e.g. Duke of Edinburgh Award Scheme, Music exams):

Certified Correct and dated   Details

[i]

Public Examinations Grades

G.C.E. Ordinary Level - The Associated Examining Board

C.S.E.   - The Yorkshire Regional Examinations Board

Grades: GCE   CSE

A ⎫
B ⎬ pass   1   pass
C ⎭   2 ⎫
                    3 ⎬
D ⎫   4 ⎭
E ⎬ fail   5 ⎫ fail
Ungraded ⎭   Ungraded ⎭

School Effort Grades:

1 - Excellent
2 - Good
3 - Satisfactory
4 - Unsatisfactory
5 - Poor

[cover, ii]

82

Example 12   (cont.)

English Skills	Staff Signature
1. Writes clearly and legibly.	
2. Grasps the basic rules of grammar.	
3. Does not make elementary spelling errors.	
4. Uses basic punctuation correctly.	
5. Can compose and structure simple sentences.	
6. Can paragraph work correctly.	
7. Can write a personal letter.	
8. Can write a business letter.	
9. Can make an accurate written report.	
10. Can make an accurate summary of a report.	
11. Shows imagination in writing.	
12. Has a wide vocabulary.	
13. Writes fluently and accurately.	
14. Can read and understand a popular newspaper.	
15. Reads with fluency.	
16. Reads widely and with interest.	
17. Can extract information from reference books.	
18. Can listen attentively and carry out oral instructions.	
19. Can give a clear spoken explanation or report.	
20. Speaks clearly and with confidence.	

[iii]

Social and Personal Qualities and Skills	Staff Signature
1. Takes a pride in his/her appearance.	
2. Is normally punctual.	
3. Is self-confident in normal daily situations.	
4. Is cooperative and helpful in school.	
5. Is cheerful and shows a sense of humour.	
6. Enjoys playing games and sports.	
7. To the best of our knowledge is honest and trustworthy.	
8. Gets on well with the great majority of fellow pupils.	
9. Has given loyal service to the school.	
10. Has held a position of responsibility at school, namely:	
11. Is courteous and well mannered.	
12. Can work well as a member of a group.	
13. Consistently makes a determined effort with his/her work.	
14. Can work well without close supervision.	
15. Can cope with work of increasing difficulty.	
16. Is at ease with adults and communicates clearly with them.	
17. Accepts authority of superiors.	
18. Conducts himself/herself with dignity and self control.	
19. Responds in a mature way to advice or criticism.	
20. Shows a capacity for organisation and leadership.	

[ii]

Example 12   (cont.)

Practical and Creative Skills

	Art	Agric.	Craft	H.Econ	Music	N.Work	Tech.St	Typing
1. Has ability in practical work.								
2. Can put theory into practice.								
3. Can work carefully and has a good standard of finish.								
4. Is able to evaluate a problem and take steps to solve it.								
5. Can produce original work.								
6. Has good coordination of hand and eye.								
7. Has appreciation of aesthetic values.								
8. Can use machinery and tools according to safety regulations.								
9. Can use basic tools and equipment competently.								
10. Can read working drawings accurately.								
11. Understands the basic elements of agriculture.								
12. Is able to perform on a musical instrument.								
13. Has a knowledge of the rudiments of music.								
14. Helpful and cooperative in carrying out the more repetitive jobs in cookery.								
15. Is able to plan, organise and prepare a family meal.								
16. Is observant and can communicate ideas clearly in drawing and painting.								
17. Can design and work accurately in Pottery/Weaving.								
18. Has a natural ability and shows artistic flair.								
19. Is able to manipulate a typewriter and use all the mechanisms fully.								
20. Is able to apply the above skill in the working of straightforward typewriting exercises.								

[v]

Maths and Science Skills

	Staff Signature
1. Can read, write and comprehend numbers.	
2. Can add/subtract/multiply/divide whole numbers.	
3. Can apply four rules to money.	
4. Understands metric/imperial system of measurement.	
5. Can handle decimals/fractions/percentages met in everyday life.	
6. Can construct/interpret tabular information/graphs.	
7. Can handle equations and simple fractions.	
8. Can perform simple speed, distance, time calculations.	
9. Can understand and use averages.	
10. Can understand and calculate perimeters/areas/volumes.	
11. Can take readings accurately.	
12. Can use basic calculator.	
13. Can use apparatus correctly, safely and work methodically.	
14. Observes carefully and records observations neatly.	
15. Can write simple account of experiments carried out.	
16. Can draw conclusions from experimental results.	
17. Can devise simple experiments to test own ideas.	
18. Can understand basic scientific principles.	
19. Can formulate and apply general principles to commonplace and familiar problems.	
20. Can assess accuracy of results and appreciate source of errors.	

[iv]

Example 12 (cont.)

Date	Achievements	Staff Signature

[vii]

PERSONAL ACHIEVEMENTS

Date	Achievements	Staff Signature

[vi]

Example 12 (cont.)

Record of Achievement

This record of the achievements and personal qualities

of

Name _____

Date of Birth _____

is certified and approved by _____

_____ Headmaster

_____ Governor

_____ Date

The above named pupil has officially left School H
and is eligible to enter full time employment

from _____ 198 .

[cover, iii]

Date	Community Service	Staff Signature

Date	Work Experience	Staff Signature

During the last two years at school, from September, 198 _____ has been absent
to _____ 198 _____
for _____ half days.

Signed _____ Educational Welfare Officer.

[viii]

Example 13 From school I (originally 8 pp A5 booklet): for convenience, p. (viii) is shown
to left of p. (i)

Name of Student:

Date of Birth:

Date of Leaving:

This Personal Achievement Record is
certified and approved by:

.... Headmaster

.... Chairman of
Governors

[i]

Achievement	Date	Staff/ Parent

[viii]

Courses Followed

Example 13 (cont.)

The following subjects have been studied during the last two years at the level shown

SUBJECT	LEVEL	Trial Exam Result	Exam Result

[ii]

PRACTICAL SKILLS

		Staff	Stamp	Date
1.	Has used simple tools safely			
2.	Can select appropriate tools			
3.	Has used basic machine tools safely			
4.	Can understand simple scientific terms			
5.	Can make and record accurate measurements or observations			
6.	Has read a meter and wired a three-pin plug			
7.	Has shown an understanding of the various types of kitchen equipment			
8.	Has planned, prepared and served a meal to a guest			
9.	Has an understanding of the importance of a balanced diet			
10.	Can type accurately at 25 w.p.m.			
11.	Can express ideas in sketch or diagram form			
12.	Can work accurately from a drawing or pattern			
13.	Shows good artistic skill			
14.	Can choose and follow a route on a map using a prismatic compass			
15.	Can produce guidance and a sketch map to assist a visitor who does not live in Cheltenham			
16.	Can use a sewing machine			

[iii]

Example 13 (cont.)   LANGUAGE SKILLS

	Staff	Stamp	Date
1. Has legible handwriting			
2. Can read and understand an article in a popular newspaper			
3. Can use simple punctuation correctly			
4. Has achieved a standard in spelling satisfactory for the teaching group			
5. Can write a personal letter			
6. Can write a formal letter			
7. Can give and take a telephone message			
8. Can accurately complete an application form			
9. Regularly borrows from the School Library			
10. Has compiled a school reading scheme folder			
11. Can make a spoken report			
12. Can follow a verbal instruction			
13. Can express facts and opinions in writing			
14. Can understand simple instructions in a foreign language			
15. Can give simple instructions in a foreign language			
16. Can write a simple letter in a foreign language			

[v]

PERSONAL AND SOCIAL SKILLS

	Staff	Stamp	Date
1. Can work well as a member of a group			
2. Takes a pride in his/her appearance			
3. Has a good attendance record			
4. Is normally punctual			
5. Enjoys playing games and sport			
6. Can swim 25m.			
7. Can work well without close supervision			
8. Can organise his/her work efficiently			
9. Understands and can apply simple first aid			
10. Has attended a school residential course or taken part in an expedition			
11. Has satisfactorily followed a child care course			
12. Has held a position of responsibility in school			
13. Can receive and escort school visitors			
14. Has shown powers of leadership			
15. Has been pleasant and well-mannered			
16. Has done a week's work experience			
17. Has been a member of a school team			

[iv]

Personal Achievements

The Student may enter here details of non-scholastic achievements, hobbies and interests, in and out of school.

Achievement	Date	Staff/Parent

[vii]

Example 13   (cont.)   **MATHS SKILLS**

	Staff	Stamp	Date
1. Understands the four rules of number			
2. Has learnt and can use times tables up to 12.			
3. Can apply the 4 rules knowledge to money and decimal fractions			
4. Has found simple fractions of given quantities of the type 1/10, ½, ¼, 1/8, 1/5			
5. Can read and understand wage tables, insurance tables and similar ready reckoner tables			
6. Has worked with metric calculations on: km, m, cm, mm, — kg, g, mg — litres, cc.			
7. Is able to measure accurately using m,cms, and mms.			
8. Has coped with areas and perimeters of a square, rectangle, triangle and circle			
9. Has covered work on the 12 and 24 hour clock systems, can tell the time and read timetables with understanding			
10. Has coped with percentages of quantities of the type 50%, 25%, 12½%, 20%, 10%, 5%, 2½%			
11. Can convert British to foreign currency and vice versa using a table or ready reckoner graph			
12. Can cope with wages, salaries, piece rates, overtime rates and commission			
13. Has covered work on Income Tax problems			
14. Is capable of using a battery operated calculator for the four basic rules			
15. Has performed calculations to find simple averages			

[vi]

REFERENCES

1. Department of Education and Science statistics, compiled for the Committee of Inquiry into the Teaching of Mathematics (chairman: Dr W.H. Cockcroft). See DES/Welsh Office, *Mathematics Counts* [Cockcroft Report], HMSO, 1982.

2. Department of Education and Science, *A View of the Curriculum* (HMI Matters for Discussion series), HMSO, 1980, p.14.

3. Board of Education, *Curriculum and Examinations in Secondary Schools*, report of the Committee of the Secondary School Examinations Council (chairman: Sir Cyril Norwood) [Norwood Report], HMSO, 1941.

4. Ministry of Education, *Secondary School Examinations other than the G.C.E.*, report of a Committee appointed by the Secondary School Examinations Council (chairman: Robert Beloe) [Beloe Report], HMSO, 1960.

5. Schools Council, *The Whole Curriculum 13-16* (Working Paper 53), Evans/Methuen Educational, 1975.

6. Department of Industry, *Engineering our Future*, report of the Committee of Inquiry into the Engineering Profession (chairman: Sir Montague Finniston) [Finniston Report], Cmnd 7794, HMSO, 1980.

7. Department of Education and Science/Scottish Office/Welsh Office, *Special Educational Needs*, report of the Committee of Enquiry into the Education of Handicapped Children and Young People (chairman: Mary Warnock) [Warnock Report], Cmnd 7212, HMSO, 1978, para. 1.4.

8. Department of Education and Science, *Aspects of Secondary Education in England*, a survey by HM Inspectors of Schools, HMSO, 1979, p.249, para. 11.3.

9. John Raven, *Education, Values and Society: the Objective of Education and the Nature and Development of Competence*, H.K. Lewis, 1977.

10. *Western Mail*, 10 July 1980.

11. *Times Higher Education Supplement*, 18 January 1980.

12. *The Times*, 12 March 1981.

13. Scottish Council for Research in Education, *Pupils in Profile* (SCRE publication 67), Hodder & Stoughton Educational, 1977.

14. Further Education Curriculum Review and Development Unit, *A Basis for Choice*, report of a Study Group on Post-16 Pre-Employment Courses (chairman: J.W. Mansell) [Mansell Report], FEU, June 1979, para. 82.

15. Tyrrell Burgess and Betty Adams, *Outcomes of Education*, Macmillan Education, 1980.

16. Patricia Broadfoot, 'Communication in the classroom: a study of the role of assessment in motivation', *Educational Review* 31 (1), 1979, p.4.

17. *Pupils in Profile* (see note 13), p.2.

18. M.N. Duffy, 'A logbook of personal achievement', *Education*, 1 February 1980, 119-20.

19. Ibid.

20. Terry Swales, *Record of Personal Achievement: an Independent Evaluation of the Swindon RPA Scheme*, Schools Council (Pamphlet 16), 1979, p.8.

21. D. Stansbury, *Record of Personal Experience, Qualities and Qualifications:* Tutor's Handbook, RPE Publications, 25 Church Street, South Brent, Devon, ?1975.

22. *Record of Personal Achievement* (see note 20).

MEMBERS OF THE MONITORING GROUP

A.H. Jennings (Chairman)   Formerly Headmaster, Ecclesfield School, Sheffield (Secondary Heads Association)

R. Aitken   Director of Education, Coventry (Association of Metropolitan Authorities)

B.C. Arthur   HM Inspectorate of Schools

J.J. Billington   Deputy Headmaster, High Pavement Sixth Form College, Nottingham (Assistant Masters and Mistresses Association)

W.S. Frearson   Ashford College, Middlesex (CSE examining boards)

J.C. Hedger   Department of Education and Science

P.M. Herbert   The Elliott School, London SW15 (National Association of Schoolmasters/Union of Women Teachers)

H.F. King   Secretary, Oxford and Cambridge Schools Examination Board (GCE examining boards)

D.I. Morgan   W.R. Tuson College, Preston, Lancs (National Union of Teachers)

R. Potts   Harraby Comprehensive School, Carlisle (National Union of Teachers)

Schools Council staff
L. Kant   Assessment and Examinations Unit